Ron Thomp

Steps to the Sermon

STEPS
TO THE
SERMON

A PLAN FOR SERMON PREPARATION

---

*by H. C. Brown, Jr., H. Gordon Clinard
and Jesse J. Northcutt*

BROADMAN PRESS • Nashville, Tennessee

ISBN: 0–8054–2103–3

4221–03

Library of Congress catalog card number: 63–19068

Printed in the United States of America

To Our Students

Preface

There are nearly as many methods of preparing sermons as there are preachers, and almost as many theories and systems of homiletics as there are teachers of homiletics and books on homiletics. Thus, the authors have wondered whether a new book should be added to an already confused picture. But creative preachers are constantly discovering improved methods, fresh principles, and varied techniques, and they are discarding the less effective. As the process of sifting and refining continues, new insights are developed. From time to time these new developments and procedures should be analyzed and published.

STEPS TO THE SERMON, an analysis of the process of sermon construction, has grown out of personal experiences, out of investigations of preaching history, out of examinations of the sermons of the masters, out of studies in rhetoric and homiletics, and out of countless discussions of preaching and of preachers. The authors believe that a *basic chronology* in this process can be defined, illustrated, and applied. To that end this book was written.

Of course, to delineate the chronology of sermon construction is not a completely new approach; other books include chapters or sections dealing with it. STEPS TO THE SERMON makes a step forward with this concept, however, in that the entire volume concerns itself with the logical order of sermon construction. This book defines, illustrates, and places in proper sequence the various homiletic items needed to build a sermon. Its purpose goes beyond the mere identification of homiletic methods, terms, and tools. Its purpose is to define, to explain, and to place in sequence all sermonic parts so that a preacher not only understands *what* he is doing and *how* he is doing it, but he understands *when* he should do it.

By following these eight steps, one will always know what to do next in building an effective sermon:

1. A prepared preacher
2. An idea to preach
3. A text interpreted
4. Related materials collected
5. Maturity secured
6. Construction completed
7. The sermon polished
8. The message preached

God speaks through a *prepared man* by giving to him a *sermon idea*. This prepared man studies his idea and relates it to a text, a thesis, and a purpose. Next, he studies the *text* until he can state the truth of the Scripture in one sentence. After Bible study the preacher examines all possible *materials* in order to give depth and breadth to the growing sermon. By allowing time for *maturity*, the preacher adds new dimensions to his developing message.

When these five basic and necessary preliminary steps have been taken, *sermon construction* begins. The preacher will state his topic or title; he then constructs the sermon body on the basis of the text, thesis, purpose, and title; he completes his organizational work by adding a conclusion, introduction, and invitation. Following this ground work the preacher *writes out his sermon* and finishes or polishes his materials. Finally he completes the task by *preaching the message*.

No claim is made that the chronological procedure of sermon building will be usable for *all* preachers nor even that it will be effective for *one* man all the time. The authors believe, however, that this approach will prove valuable and usable for most preachers most of the time.

Many scholars in homiletics and related subjects have significantly influenced this book. Among them are John A. Broadus, Edwin C. Dargan, H. E. Dana, Andrew W. Blackwood, H.

Grady Davis, Webb Garrison, and Donald G. Miller. The men who were classroom teachers of the authors, Jesse B. Weatherspoon, Vernon L. Stanfield, Jeff D. Ray, and G. Earl Guinn, teach again on almost every page.

We are grateful for the encouragement which has come from many friends of the faculty and administration of Southwestern Baptist Theological Seminary. Andrew W. Blackwood, professor emeritus, Princeton Theological Seminary; James W. Cox, associate professor of preaching, Southern Baptist Theological Seminary; and Vernon L. Stanfield, professor of preaching, New Orleans Baptist Theological Seminary, read the manuscript and made valuable suggestions.

Many have worked faithfully to assist us in the preparation of the manuscript. Our secretaries, Nannie Don Beaty, Jean Fleming, Mary Duren, and Mrs. Mary Douglas, helped at many points. Mary Pruitt has been kind and devoted in the final typing. Many others gave counsel and encouragement in the production of this which we hope will be a helpful guide to many young ministers in their preparation as "heralds" of the eternal Word of God.

Contents

I
Understanding the Task

God chooses and uses men in his kingdom as he wills. In the beginning of the Hebrew nation the Lord said to Moses: "Come now therefore, and I will send thee unto Pharaoh, that thou mayest bring forth my people the children of Israel out of Egypt" (Ex. 3:10). During the development of the kingdom God chose Samuel. "The Lord came, and stood, and called as at other times, Samuel, Samuel. Then Samuel answered, Speak; for thy servant heareth" (1 Sam. 3:10).

In the eighth century B.C. God spoke to Amos:

The lion hath roared, who will not fear? the Lord God hath spoken, who can but prophesy? Then answered Amos, and said to Amaziah, I was no prophet, neither was I a prophet's son; but I was an herdman, and a gatherer of sycomore fruit: And the Lord took me as I followed the flock, and the Lord said unto me, Go, prophesy unto my people Israel (Amos 3:8; 7:14-15).

Later the Lord called Isaiah, the prince of prophets: "Also I heard the voice of the Lord, saying, Whom shall I send, and who will go for us? Then said I, Here am I; send me" (Isa. 6:8).

Jesus, in his earthly ministry, also called out men. "Jesus, walking by the sea of Galilee, saw two brethren, Simon called Peter, and Andrew his brother, casting a net into the sea: for they were fishers. And he saith unto them, Follow me, and I will make you fishers of men" (Matt. 4:18-19).

Was it not also true when "Bible days" had passed and post-New Testament times had begun that God continued to call men? There were Origen, Augustine, Chrysostom, and Ambrose in the early centuries. There were Bernard, Francis, Dominic,

2 STEPS TO THE SERMON

Wycliffe, Huss, and Savonarola after the Dark Ages and before
the Reformation. There were Luther, Calvin, Zwingli, Latimer,
and Knox during the Reformation. There were Wesley, Whitefield, Bunyan, Baxter, Spurgeon, Maclaren, Edwards, Brooks,
Beecher, Broadus, and Moody in more recent centuries. And in
the first half of the twentieth century there were Sunday, Scar-
borough, Truett, Gossip, Stewart, Chappell, Fosdick, Buttrick,
and Sockman.

As surely as God called the prophets, apostles, and great
preachers of history, he calls men today. As always, the basis of
God's call is still dependent upon the will, the good pleasure, of
the Lord. In Mark 3:13-14 (ASV) the sovereignty of Jesus is
depicted as he called out and sent forth the apostles: "He goeth
up into the mountain, and calleth unto him whom he himself
would; and they went unto him. And he appointed twelve, that
they might be with him, and that he might send them forth to
preach."

An era of decadent Christianity will be upon us if the belief
in a divine call is lost. The Dark Ages will again envelop the
churches if men cease to believe in and respond to the call of
God. There can be no powerful or positive or effective preaching apart from a God-called ministry.

The man God uses to preach the unsearchable riches of the
Lord Jesus Christ is a regenerate person. Spurgeon was horrified
by the idea that an unregenerate person should attempt to preach
the gospel to lost men.

How horrible to be a preacher of the gospel and yet to be uncon-
verted! Let each man here whisper to his own inmost soul,
"What a dreadful thing it will be *for me* if I should be ignorant of
the power of the truth which I am preparing to proclaim!" Un-
converted ministry involves the most unnatural relationships. A
graceless pastor is a blind man elected to a professorship of optics,
philosophizing upon light and vision, discoursing upon and dis-
tinguishing to others the nice shades and delicate blendings of the
prismatic colours, while he himself is absolutely in the dark! He
is a dumb man elevated to the chair of music; a deaf man fluent

upon symphonies and harmonies! He is a mole professing to edu-
cate eaglets; a limpet elected to preside over angels.[1]

The man God uses to preach the gospel is a committed man.
All that the preacher discerns within and about himself must
be committed to the Lord. Whether it be his public or private
life and thoughts, whether it be his personality resources of
moral and ethical concepts, or mental powers, or emotional
resources, or of physical capacities—he must commit each of
these to the Lord's unrestricted use. Moreover, in all of his relationships—with parents, wife, children, friends, church members, associates, and strangers—he must conduct himself as a
consecrated man. No personality trait, resource, relationship, or
obligation can be placed beyond the control and care of the
Lord who saved him and called him.

The man God calls to preach eternal truth is a man who constantly communes with the Lord. No man preaches any better
than he prays. No man can rise higher in his preaching of the
gospel than he can rise in his private and family spiritual life.

Every possible evidence bears testimony that a minister must
sustain a close fellowship with God if he would thrive spiritually. The dramatically beautiful fellowship of Christ with the
Father bears witness to the necessity of a consistent devotional
life. Later, in the midst of mounting responsibility and multiply-
ing tasks, the apostles cried for relief that they might give themselves more completely to preaching and to spiritual affairs.
The writings of Paul abound in references to "praying without
ceasing," "giving thanks without ceasing," and "remembering
without ceasing." Paul lived his life in the white heat of an
intense fellowship with God. Through the ages the most effective servants of the Lord have been those who have nourished
their souls in close fellowship with him. Without exception
every preacher of great power has had intimate communion
with the Lord.

---

[1] Charles H. Spurgeon, *Lectures to My Students* (New ed.; Grand Rapids:
Zondervan Publishing House, 1955), pp. 9-10.

While it is imperative that a preacher be a truly regenerated Christian, be called of God to a preaching ministry, and grow continually in fellowship with God, he must also prepare himself through diligent study if he is to be an effective spokesman to his age. Before one can prepare and preach effective sermons, he should develop an understanding of his basic task as it relates to the nature of preaching, the status of preaching, the objectives of preaching, and the history of preaching.

The Nature of Preaching

Although the New Testament offers no formal definition of preaching, a study of the primary terms reveals much about the nature of preaching. The most frequently used word in the New Testament for preaching, *keryssein*, is translated "to proclaim" or "to herald" and occurs more than fifty times in its various inflections. In the Gospels and in Acts it is usually translated "preach" or "preaching" or "preached." It denotes that the messenger has a message of authority from another. Of course, in the New Testament sense, the messenger has a message from God about Christ, and since the messenger is divinely appointed, the hearers are obligated to hear and to obey.

Another important New Testament term for preaching, *euangelizesthai*, is translated "to preach good tidings or good news." This word indicates the nature of the message as good news—good news of something to come or of something that has come and is available.

Throughout the New Testament many other words are used to indicate the act of "preaching" even though the specific word "preaching" is not always used. Four such words are *didaskein*, "to impart divine truth through teaching"; *dialegesthai*, "to discourse or reason with others with a view to persuasion"; *lalein*, "to talk or to discourse"; and *parakalein*, "to call to one's side or to admonish."

"Preaching" is evidently used in the New Testament in the most general sense, as signifying a heralding in every manner and mode of the word of God to man, to one man as well as to the people.

Preaching thus is not necessarily a popular address, or a regular discourse in a regular assembly, but may be applied to all kinds of "proclaiming" or "publishing" of Christian truth in whatever way, in private conversation, in the interviews of missionaries with the heathen, in the addresses of evangelists, in the common intercourse of men . . . it is making known in any and every effectual way, by one's conduct, precept, or personality, the message of God to men.[2]

Through the years many have attempted to define the nature of preaching in precise terms. Perhaps the best known definition was set out by Phillips Brooks in 1877: "What, then, is preaching of which we are to speak? It is not hard to find a definition. Preaching is the communication of truth by man to men. It has in it two essential elements, truth and personality. Neither of those can it spare and still be preaching."[3]

In the first sentences of his excellent book, *The Making of the Sermon*, T. Harwood Pattison adds a new dimension to the definition of preaching—that of persuasion.

Preaching is the spoken communication of divine truth with a view to persuasion. Accepting this as a sufficient definition, we notice that it covers the three points with which we are chiefly concerned in a sermon, namely: its matter, its manner, and its purpose. As to the matter of this communication, it is "divine truth." This tells us what to preach. As to the manner of this communication, it is divine truth "spoken." This tells us how to preach. As to the purpose of this communication, it is divine truth spoken "with a view to persuasion." This tells us why we preach.[4]

Andrew W. Blackwood, the dean of American teachers of preaching, draws his definition of preaching from a study of outstanding preaching of the past.

[2] James M. Hoppin, *Homiletics* (New York: Funk & Wagnalls Co., 1883), p. 10.

[3] *Lectures on Preaching* (London: Griffith, Farrar & Co., 1877), p. 5.

[4] *The Making of the Sermon* (Philadelphia: The American Baptist Publication Society, 1898), p. 3.

What do we understand by preaching? It means divine truth through personality or the truth of God voiced by a chosen personality to meet human needs. . . .

From another point of view preaching calls for the interpretation of life today in light that comes from God today, largely through the Scriptures.[5]

The current emphasis on the nature of preaching centers largely on theological concepts which have been reborn in a rising tide of studies in biblical theology. This new thrust finds Karl Barth, H. H. Farmer, Emil Brunner, I. T. Jones, Richard Cammerer, Robert Mounce, and Donald Miller discussing preaching as an existential encounter, a redemptive deed, and a divine act. Early in the twentieth century, P. T. Forsyth declared: "With preaching Christianity stands or falls because it is the declaration of a Gospel. Nay more—far more—it is the Gospel prolonging and declaring itself." [6]

Donald G. Miller, in a recent book, *Fire in Thy Mouth*, captures the essence of recent biblical and theological views concerning preaching when he writes:

To preach the gospel . . . is not merely to say words but to effect a deed. To preach is not merely to stand in a pulpit and speak, no matter how eloquently and effectively, nor even to set forth a theology, no matter how clearly it is stated nor how worthy the theology. To preach is to become a part of a dynamic event wherein the living, redeeming God reproduces his act of redemption in a living encounter with men through the preacher. True preaching is an extension of the Incarnation into the contemporary moment, the transfiguring of the Cross and the Resurrection from ancient facts of a remote past into living realities of the present. A sermon is an act wherein the crucified, risen Lord personally confronts men either to save or to judge them. . . . In a real sermon, then, Christ is the Preacher. The Preacher speaks through the preacher.[7]

---

[5] *The Preparation of Sermons* (New York: Abingdon-Cokesbury Press, 1948), p. 13.

[6] *Positive Preaching and the Modern Mind* (New York: George H. Doran Co., 1907), p. 5.

[7] *Fire in Thy Mouth* (New York: Abingdon Press, 1954), p. 17.

Robert H. Mounce in his helpful work *The Essential Nature of New Testament Preaching* expresses a similar conviction: "Preaching is that timeless link between God's great redemptive Act and man's apprehension of it. It is the medium through which God contemporizes His historic Self-disclosure and offers man the opportunity to respond in faith." [8]

Such views speak strongly concerning the importance of preaching by insisting that the Word of God cannot be separated from its proclamation; that the gospel is in fact a preached gospel; that preaching is the redemptive event in contemporary time; that the act of preaching is part of God's encounter with man; that preaching is not merely a means of conveying content, but is in a real sense bound up with the content; that it is part of God's saving activity; and that it is God's means of giving life to men. If these statements be true, all must admit to the supreme importance of preaching.

While agreeing with this contemporary emphasis, John R. Stott warns against careless terminology in setting out the existential nature of preaching. He calls attention, in examining the views of Mounce, to the various statements concerning the transference of the events of the past into the contemporary moment and then tries to place these expressions in correct focus.

I confess that I find some of this language loose and perilous. In what sense can the herald by his proclamation 'prolong' or effect an 'extension' or 'continuance' of God's redemptive act in the cross? Dr. Mounce seems to indicate that in some way the cross is 'once again taking place.' At least he uses this expression twice. . . .

What Dr. Mounce and other writers are really saying, I believe— with which I heartily agree—is that it is by preaching that God makes past history a present reality. The cross was, and will always remain, a unique historical event of the past. And there it will remain, in the past, in the books, unless God Himself makes it real and relevant to men today. It is by preaching, in which He makes His appeal to men through men, that God accomplishes this miracle. He

[8] Grand Rapids: Wm. B. Eerdmans Publishing Co., 1960, p. 153.

opens their eyes to see its true meaning, its eternal value and its abiding merit. . . .

God not only *confronts* men through the preacher's proclamation; He actually *saves* men through it as well. This St. Paul states categorically: 'Since, in the wisdom of God, the world did not know God through wisdom, it pleased God through the folly of the *kerygma* to save those who believe' (1 Cor. 1:21). Similarly, the gospel is itself 'the power of God unto salvation to every one that believeth' (Rom. 1:16, AV). Did not Jesus in the Nazareth Synagogue, quoting from Isaiah 61, say: 'The Spirit of the Lord is upon me, because He has anointed me to preach good news to the poor. He has sent me to proclaim release to the captives and recovering of sight to the blind, to set at liberty those who are oppressed'? (Lk. 4:18). His mission, He says, is not only 'to proclaim release to the captives' but actually 'to set' them 'at liberty!' [9]

New Testament preaching, according to Stott, was unique in that while it proclaimed life, it gave life. Since this was true, preaching was supremely important in the New Testament.

In view of the various facets of preaching found through a study of the Greek words for preaching, an examination of various opinions concerning preaching, and a look at the contemporary insights about preaching, what is preaching in terms of today? *Preaching is the effective communication of divine truth, as contained in the Christian Scriptures, by a man called of God to witness for him to a redemptive deed for the purpose of giving eternal life through Jesus Christ.*

The Status of Preaching

In view of the New Testament and contemporary theological emphasis on the importance of preaching, it comes as a surprise to discover that preaching is largely in eclipse in the mid-twentieth century.[10] Evidence abounds that preaching is in a deplor-

---

[9] *The Preacher's Portrait in the New Testament* (Grand Rapids: Wm. B. Eerdmans Publishing Co., 1961), pp. 52-54.

[10] Portions of this section first appeared in "Power in the Pulpit," H. C. Brown, Jr., *Christianity Today* (January 2, 1961), 7-8. Used by permission.

able condition and that preachers are seriously confused about their basic responsibility. Donald G. Miller cites an unknown critic of preaching who said, "if Protestantism ever dies with a dagger in its back, the dagger will be the Protestant sermon." [11]

The Discrediting of Preaching

Miller sees contempt for the task of preaching on the part of some preachers as one reason for the present deplorable status of preaching. He cites an excerpt from a letter written by a ministerial student: "I consider preaching as a necessary evil. I shall do as much of it as my position demands in order to qualify for the other more important tasks on which my heart is set. But I could well wish to avoid preaching almost entirely." [12]

That the world heaps criticism upon the task of preaching is seen as further evidence of the present confused state of preaching. "The discrediting of preaching is one of the marks of our time. 'Don't preach at me!' is an expression which suggests that by many preaching is held in contempt." [13]

Neither the minority voice of a confused student nor the strident criticism of a critical world would be so damaging were it not for the tragic fact that many capable preachers give support to such views by holding commonplace convictions about the task of preaching. That no sense of conviction or assurance about the minister's work hangs over the American pulpit is the studied judgment of Webb Garrison in his significant book *The Preacher and His Audience*. Halford E. Luccock reports that many ministers conduct themselves after the fashion of H. G. Wells's croquet player who said:

I don't care. The world may be going to pieces. The Stone Age may be returning. This may . . . be the sunset of civilization. I'm sorry, but I can't help it this morning. I have other engagements. . . . I am going to play croquet with my aunt at half past twelve today. [14]

---

[11] *The Way to Biblical Preaching* (New York: Abingdon Press, 1957), p. 7.
[12] *Fire in Thy Mouth*, p. 14.   [13] *Ibid.*, p. 13.
[14] *In the Minister's Workshop* (New York: Abingdon-Cokesbury Press, 1944), p. 43.

Others find cause for alarm about preaching today in the "clown complex" occasionally found in some ministers. Because rhetoricians, statesmen, politicians, salesmen, and preachers have known for centuries that humor can be and is a devastatingly effective speech weapon, some men have wrongly and tragically elevated humor to the first place of importance among homiletical devices. It is important that preachers refrain from playing the role of court clown and that they live the role for which they have been divinely commissioned—the role of prophet for the King of kings.

Perhaps the most serious evidence concerning the low estate of preaching in the mid-twentieth century is the confusion of roles which plagues the modern preacher. The major question facing some ministers as they arise in the morning is "Who am I today?" Pierce Harris wrote in the *Atlanta Journal:*

The modern preacher has to make as many visits as a country doctor, shake as many hands as a politician, prepare as many briefs as a lawyer, see as many people as a specialist. He has to be as good an executive as the president of a university, and as good a financier as a bank president, and in the midst of it all, he has to be so good a diplomat that he could umpire a baseball game between the knights of Columbus and the Ku Klux Klan.[15]

Samuel W. Blizzard, after a two-year period of research and investigation, discovered some interesting facts concerning the roles of ministers.[16] Attempting to find the preacher's image of himself, he asked thirteen hundred ministers to arrange six roles or functions—preacher, pastor, priest, teacher, organizer, and administrator—in the order of importance according to their conception of an ideal pattern. The more than seven hundred who replied felt that the minister is: (1) a preacher, (2) a pastor, (3) a priest, (4) a teacher, (5) an organizer, (6) an admin-

[15] Used by permission of Pierce Harris and the *Atlanta Journal.*
[16] See "The Roles of the Rural Parish Minister, the Protestant Seminaries, and the Sciences of Social Behavior," *Religious Education* (November-December, 1955), 383-92; as well as other articles by Blizzard.

istrator. Blizzard also asked them to arrange the same six roles functionally, according to the amount of time they spent performing these roles. The results were: (1) administrator, (2) pastor, (3) priest, (4) organizer, (5) preacher, (6) teacher.

During an average work day of ten and one-half hours these men spent an average of only thirty-eight minutes preparing to preach. The time spent on administration was seven times more than that spent on preaching. These men declared that preaching ought to be their primary function, but they had reduced it to a very weak fifth-rate role in actual performance.

The Renaissance of Preaching

In spite of the present low estate of preaching, signs of hope are present which indicate a renaissance of preaching. One sign of this awakening is that preaching is receiving a strong emphasis in American seminaries.

An investigation of theological education reported preaching to be one of five departments common to twenty-five seminaries in 1935. In 1955 Niebuhr, Williams, and Gustafson found that there were still only five departments common to the same twenty-five seminaries. One conclusion was that "the 'classical' disciplines [of theological education], Bible, Church History, Theology, Pastoral Care, and Preaching, must certainly be included in any theological curriculum." [17]

Another sign of an awakening as to the importance of preaching is that some outstanding preachers dare to lock their office doors in order to pray, to study, and to prepare sermons. They are encouraged to believe that when they find messages from the Lord, people will rejoice to hear those messages. They dare to believe that people will excuse them from many aimless activities which plague the modern preacher if they are busy finding God's message.

Another sign of a renaissance in preaching is the heart-hunger

---

[17] H. Richard Niebuhr, Daniel Day Williams, and James M. Gustafson, *The Advancement of Theological Education* (New York: Harper & Bros., 1957), p. 86.

of laymen for pastors who preach the Word. Again and again laymen have volunteered their convictions that ministers should pray more, study more, and rightly divide the word of truth. Jesse Johnson, an attorney in Richmond, Virginia, has said:

> To my mind, the first and greatest work of the man in the pulpit is to preach the Word. If God has called him at all, He has called him to do just that. Nothing else should come before it. Nothing else can take its place. Almost every other work in the church can be accomplished by laymen or laywomen, but preaching is still the preacher's job.[18]

Moreover, let the minister take hope in facts often overlooked in analyzing Blizzard's report. While it is true that Blizzard has pointed up an alarming neglect of preaching on the part of preachers, it is also true that he has presented documentary proof that all the pressures, programs, and problems of the preachers have not been able to convince them that preaching is not their primary task. Ministers still believe that they are preachers first of all.

The Primacy of Preaching

In view of the prominence of preaching in the New Testament and in the writings of scholars in the field of homiletics, Bible, and theology, and in view of the many encouraging signs pointing to a renaissance of preaching, what should the modern minister do about preaching? *He should re-emphasize the primacy of preaching.*

Of course the minister has many other tasks and functions, but to have a ministry where "preaching is primary" means that the most important thing that a minister can do in the course of his week's work is to preach, to speak for God. As he prepares and preaches, so is he qualified to perform his other major functions.

---

[18] "A Modern Prophet" in *Messages for Men*, ed. H. C. Brown, Jr. (Grand Rapids: Zondervan Publishing House, 1960), p. 88.

To have a ministry where preaching is primary may or may not mean that the minister is a great man, or that he is a great orator, or that he has a magnetic personality, but it does mean that he will have profound convictions about the importance of preaching. The primacy of preaching means that a man called of God will take the stance of a prophet to see and speak for God. It means that he will be faithful as a herald to get and to speak the message of the King, and it means that he will speak only the King's message.

To have a ministry where preaching is primary means that a preacher's attitude, his philosophy, his perspective, his stance before God is like that of Amos, Isaiah, Peter, and Paul. The content of his message will be the gospel proclaimed; it will be the gospel theologically interpreted; it will be the gospel applied. To have a ministry where preaching is primary means that the preacher will preach a pure gospel for a holy God.

In giving first place to the preaching aspect of his ministry, the modern preacher has ample and notable precedent in the prophets of the Old Testament and also in the ministry of our Lord.

The instruction and example of our Lord cannot be disregarded and is as clear as the sun. For the preaching of the gospel He came, and for its high purpose was He born. "And he said unto them, Let us go into the next towns, that I may preach there also: for therefore came I forth" (Mark 1:38).[19]

About our Lord's visit to the synagogue in Nazareth, Luke recorded:

And he opened the book, and found the place where it was written,
The Spirit of the Lord is upon me,
Because he anointed me to preach good tidings to the poor:
He hath sent me to proclaim release to the captives,

[19] James W. Clarke, *Dynamic Preaching* (Westwood, N.J.: Fleming H. Revell Co., 1960), pp. 25-26.

And recovering of sight to the blind,
To set at liberty them that are bruised,
To proclaim the acceptable year of the Lord.
And he closed the book, and gave it back to the attendant, and sat
down: and the eyes of all in the synagogue were fastened on him.
And he began to say unto them, To-day hath this scripture been
fulfilled in your ears (Luke 4:17-21, ASV).

Jesus testified boldly that he was anointed to preach and to
proclaim. It appears to be distinctly true that of the three basic
tasks of Jesus—teaching, healing, and preaching—preaching was
primary. He had come to preach; healing was secondary.

Not only was preaching primary to the prophets and to
Jesus, it was also primary to the apostles. Luke's record of apostolic conviction at this point is clearly shown in Acts 6:14. In
this account is found the record of the selection of the seven to
help with the business affairs of the church. The apostles wanted
to give attention to prayer and to the ministry of the word. The
twelve did not minimize the ministry of table serving, for they
had been serving tables, but they said that for them there was
another ministry which took priority. They would have agreed
with a recent writer who said that "the preaching of the word
is prior or it is too late." [20]

Even though they were often stubborn, slow to learn,
greedy, and contentious, they learned most of their lessons well.
By their observation of the actions of their Lord and by their
understanding of his commands, they believed preaching to be
primary for them. Simon Peter told Cornelius that the risen
Lord had commanded them to preach to the people (Acts
10:42). "The early preachers were not of the elite; not many
great, not many wise, not many mighty. But the lowliest of
them had nobler things to tell than Plato ever dreamed, Aris-
totle ever argued, or Socrates ever discussed." [21]

The unrivaled message was to be given to the world through

---

[20] *Ibid.*, p. 32
[21] *Ibid.*, pp. 28-29.

preaching. For "how shall they hear without a preacher?" asked Paul (Rom. 10:14). And to his young protege, Paul admonished: "Preach the word, be urgent in season . . . convince, rebuke, and exhort" (2 Tim. 4:2, RSV). To Titus he declared firmly, God "hath in due times manifested his word through preaching" (Titus 1:3).

Only when God's chosen servant comes to a true understanding of the nature of preaching and discovers that preaching should be primary in his ministry, will he devote the proper time and attention to it. When he attains this state of understanding and performance, he will walk after the noble example of the prophets, the apostles, and the Lord Jesus Christ.

The Objectives of Preaching

An understanding of the objectives of preaching is essential in the preacher's preparation. An objective is that on which one sets his mind and heart as a purpose, goal, or result. The term "objective," as applied to preaching, includes both the overall or total purpose of a preacher's ministry and that of the immediate sermon he is preparing. (The material in this section has been greatly influenced by Dr. J. B. Weatherspoon, who is planning a volume on the objectives of preaching.)

The Total Objective

The total objective (also called the ultimate, supreme, or comprehensive objective) is to bring *life* to the people. A minister ought to see clearly the difference between what he is trying to do with the twenty-four hours of today and what he is trying to do with the forty or more years of his ministry. Today he may be preparing a sermon on "total stewardship" in which he pleads for stronger financial support for God's kingdom. His aim is to increase the income of the church. Such a limited purpose would hardly suffice as a supreme goal.

Nothing less than the purpose of Christ will be sufficient for the dedicated preacher. "The thief cometh not, but that he may steal, and kill, and destroy: I came that they may have life, and may have it abundantly" (John 10:10, ASV). In this comprehensive purpose for his own ministry Jesus directs his ministers to the only goal worthy of dedicated men—life for the people.

Life, a term so rich, so profound, and yet so simple, embraces life eternal for tomorrow and life abundant for today. With *life* as a guide the minister will be able to shape his preaching, to plan his pastoral care, and to control his emphasis on organizations. There need never be an unbalanced ministry if the pastor knows that his ultimate purpose is to see that those persons placed by God under his care have life.

The Major Objectives

While the total objective is life, there are immediate goals which must be formulated for individual sermons. The immediate goals or major objectives are determined by the needs of the people. Within each congregation are six basic needs. People need to be *saved*, to grow in *devotion* to God, to develop more mature *understanding* of God's truth, to live in *better relationship* with others, to *serve God* in a more dedicated way, and to *find strength* and comfort in trouble. Every sermon should be designed to meet one of these basic areas of need.

The evangelistic objective.—The presence of unsaved people in the congregation or in the community necessitates the evangelistic or gospel objective. It comprises more than any one or several truths about God. Evangelistic preaching presents the gospel—the good news—to those who do not know or who have not accepted it by faith.

The devotional objective.—The devotional objective or the goal of love is directed toward Christians with the ideal of causing them to love, to adore, and to worship God. General themes, such as prayer, praise, thanksgiving, joy and beauty of faith, the majesty and holiness of God, are useful in motivating Christians to adore and worship the Lord.

The doctrinal objective.—The doctrinal objective is used when a keen discernment of God and his truth is needed. Christians constantly need assistance in grappling with the great and noble truths of the faith. As the pastor searches for relevant messages, he will be mindful of the difficulty his people have in comprehending God's nature, Christ's birth, the cross, regeneration, the resurrection, and the second coming. Numerous other themes which clarify insight and belief furnish the preacher a challenge for doctrinal preaching. *The doctrinal goal is a distinct goal when used alone, and it is a servant of the other goals when used with them.*

The ethical objective.—The ethical objective presents a creative challenge in almost any age but especially in the twentieth century. At the point where a converted person touches the life of another person, there Christian ethics operate. True Christian ethics is grounded in a saved man's relationship to God, but it expresses itself in every area of life—in family relations, in business contacts, in public schools, in politics, in the armed forces, and in race relations. A Christian should have such an effective ethical relationship to God and to his neighbor that his neighbor will desire to know God. The need of the congregation for proper relationships with the Lord and with neighbors may be met by effective ethical preaching.

The consecrative objective.—The consecrative or actional objective meets the need of God's children to be fully committed to him. Some need to hear the voice of God calling them to a life of unconditional surrender in the local church. The consecrative objective challenges the pastor to lead his people to dedicate to God all the resources under their control, including time, talent, and personality.

A "promotional objective" is sometimes listed separately but can be discussed more helpfully with the consecrative objective. Occasionally the pastor finds it necessary to "promote" a building project or an organizational program or some other institutional aspect of the church. By considering the promotional objective as a part of the consecrative purpose, the pastor can elevate his attitudes and methods in promotional work.

The supportive objective.—The supportive or pastoral objective is born of the sufferings and burdens of people in trouble.

That men, women, and children do need grace and the everlasting arms of God is undeniable. In using the supportive objective, the pastor will find a *life situation* in his congregation which requires spiritual comfort, and he will address himself to it. There is spiritual joy in ministering to people in need, but the pastor must beware of creating artificial situations which require attention and of devoting all of his attention to this area of need.

The Specific Objective

After one of the six basic areas of need has been chosen as the major goal, it is necessary to formulate a specific objective for the immediate sermon. The specific objective expresses in a positive or affirmative statement the response the pastor desires from his congregation as a result of one particular sermon. Always the specific objective is part of the total objective—*life* for the people. Furthermore, it is a facet of one of the six major objectives. The specific objective relates directly to *one* aspect of *one* major objective in *one* sermon to *one* audience on *one* occasion. For example, in preaching to his own congregation on an October Sunday morning in regard to the budget campaign, a preacher might have as his ultimate objective, abundant life; as his major objective, the consecrative goal; and as his specific objective, that each church member should tithe.

The total, major, and specific objectives are closely related. They represent the development of purpose from the general to the particular. In helping the preacher to pinpoint his thoughts, they constitute three steps to effective messages which can be clearly comprehended.

The History of Preaching

Origins of Christian Preaching

Three streams—ancient oratory, Hebrew prophecy, and the Christian gospel—comprise the sources of Christian preaching.[22]

---

[22] E. C. Dargan, *A History of Preaching* (New York: George H. Doran Co., 1905), I, 14. This volume is the principal source in this section.

Ancient oratory and Hebrew prophecy flowed separately for hundreds of years, and by the third century A.D. these two merged with the Christian gospel to produce Christian preaching.

Ancient oratory.—The precise origin of oratory is not known. It is commonly assumed that oratory followed the development of languages which grew out of a common ancestry.[23] In the development of oratory the contributions of the ancient civilizations and the early Hebrews were few in comparison to the later work of the Greeks, Romans, and Hebrew prophets. Early civilized nations such as Egypt, Assyria, and Persia contributed little because of totalitarian types of governments which discouraged free speech. Oratory was not unknown among these peoples, but it never reached a high level of development.

Among the Hebrew people, before the time of the great prophets, several examples of ancient oratory can be found. "The speech of Judah before Joseph, is unsurpassed in all literature as an example of the simplest, tenderest, truest pathos." [24] The author of Job was well-acquainted with oratory. The marvelous farewell speech of Moses is found in the book of Deuteronomy. Other examples of Old Testament speeches may be found in Judges 9, 1 Samuel 24, 25, and 26.

The major contributions to ancient oratory came through Greco-Roman rhetoric. It was in the fertile minds of the Greeks that oratory as a mental discipline was developed:

Ancient eloquence, on its secular and artistic side, reached its culmination among this gifted and versatile people. The speeches in the Homeric Poems show that in the earliest, semi-mythical times the Greeks employed and prized the gift of eloquence. The growth of political freedom, the early and vigorous development of dialectic philosophy, the cultivation and excellence of art and literature, along with the imaginative and lively intellect and the flexible and

[23] A. T. Robertson and W. Hersey Davis, *A New Short Grammar of the Greek Testament* (New York: Harper & Bros., 1931), pp. 3-6.
[24] John A. Broadus, *Lectures on the History of Preaching* (New York: A. C. Armstrong & Son, 1876), p. 6.

powerful language of the Greeks, all contributed to their marvellous
and abiding attainments in the field of oratory.[25]

It is thought that the rules of rhetoric were first formulated
by Korax in 466 B.C.[26] After Thrasybulus, ruler of Syracuse,
who had confiscated private lands, was overthrown, private
property was restored to the citizens through court action.
Claimants were required to appear in court and present data
concerning their confiscated property. Confusion reigned. Most
of the citizens were ignorant of proper procedures, and out of
the chaos came the rules of Korax. He taught that five items
were needed in making a speech: proem (introduction), presentation of facts, argument, secondary remarks, and peroration
(conclusion). The art of rhetoric proved to be extremely useful
and developed rapidly in the centuries following Korax.

As Greece conquered the world by force, it also conquered
the minds of men with its educational procedures. Greek educational methods, schools, and rhetoric flowed out to the ends
of the earth. Even though Rome later conquered the Greek
Empire, Grecian rhetoric and education conquered the Roman
mind. As God later used the universal Greek language for writing the New Testament, he also used Greco-Roman rhetoric as
an instrument for proclaiming his gospel.

In spite of the impact of rhetoric on the proclamation of the
gospel in the centuries following Christ, the art of rhetoric
lacked moral and religious content essential to the highest eloquence. The impact of rhetoric on Christianity was chiefly at
the point of form and mechanics of preaching. The moral void
in rhetoric was adequately filled by Hebrew prophecy.

Hebrew prophecy.—The long and glorious history of Hebrew
prophecy prepared the way for Christian preaching. The Bible
records that Enoch (Jude 14), Noah (2 Peter 2:5), Isaac (Gen.
27:27-29), Jacob (Gen. 49:3-27), Moses (throughout Deuter-

---

[25] Dargan, *op. cit.,* I, 16.
[26] E. C. Dargan, *The Art of Preaching in the Light of Its History* (Nashville:
Sunday School Board of the Southern Baptist Convention, 1922), p. 30.

onomy), and Joshua (Josh. 23-24) prophesied or spoke words
of counsel from the Lord. Later Samuel, Nathan, Elijah, Elisha,
Amos, Hosea, Joel, Micah, Isaiah, Jeremiah, Ezekiel, Daniel, and
Malachi heard God speak and related his messages to Israel.

The prophets attributed their ability to discern and to describe events to the belief that God had called them and placed
his words in their mouth. Although much emphasis has been
placed on their ability to see and to describe *the future,* in all
probability the prophets' primary function was to see and to tell
God's message to Israel for the day in which they lived. The
Hebrew words for *prophet* emphasize two ideas: the ability
"to see" for the Lord, and the ability "to speak" in a warm and
fervent manner in his name. The prophets did predict, but basically they were forthtellers rather than foretellers.

From the period of the great prophets to the restoration following the Exile, the nature of prophecy changed very little.
But in this latter period came the development of something
which was to influence preaching profoundly in the years to
come, *i.e.,* the regular exposition of the Old Testament Scriptures as a vital part of the synagogue services of worship. The
exact date of the origin of the synagogue is not known, but it
seems to have been some time during the Exile. While captives
in a heathen land, cut off from Temple worship, the Israelites
probably devised the synagogue system. When the refugees
returned to Palestine, they established synagogues in almost
every town.[27] In that era the age of prophecy ended, and a long
night came as the Promised One was awaited.

Without question the synagogue system had profound influence on subsequent religious development. When Christ sent
forth his disciples with a new message, they found a people
already trained in hearing the exposition of God's Word in a
special place set apart for sacred discourse. Moreover, the synagogue later afforded the apostles preaching places in almost
every city in the world. The general structure of the synagogue

---

[27] T. Harwood Pattison, *The History of Christian Preaching* (Philadelphia:
American Baptist Publication Society, 1903), p. 9.

building, the type of service, the use of Scripture for divine instruction influenced Christian preaching for all time.

The Christian gospel.—The third stream of Christian preaching, the Christian gospel, is found in the ministries of John the Baptist, of Jesus Christ, and of the apostles. John the Baptist, the link between the Old Testament and the New, came out of the wilderness, proclaiming the coming of the Promised One and declaring that the kingdom of heaven was at hand. John laid the foundation for the unfolding of the gospel.

In the coming of Jesus the cornerstone of Christian preaching was laid. He was the burden of his own message as he unfolded to the disciples the good news about the kingdom of God. Jesus himself was a preacher, and to preaching he devoted much of his energy. Not only did Christ make preaching important in his own country but he commanded his disciples to preach (Matt. 10). It is significant that in his final meeting with his church, he spoke about preaching: "Go ye into all the world, and preach the gospel to the whole creation" (Mark 16:15, ASV).

In the main the sources of apostolic preaching were in the Old Testament as it had been opened to them by Christ, from the experiences they had with Jesus, from the events centering in Jesus himself, and from the individual interpretations the preachers gave to the total picture. To the apostles and the disciples "gospel" and "preaching" were virtually equivalent terms. "Gospel" was very often the direct object of the verb "to preach." Indeed, the connection of ideas is so close that *keryssein* [to proclaim] by itself can be used as a virtual equivalent for *euangelizesthai*, "to evangelize," or "to preach the Gospel."[28]

From the preaching of the apostles some New Testament scholars have drawn a sharp distinction between the *kerygma*, or gospel, and the *didaché*, or ethical instruction. Other scholars point out, however, that there is not so much a sharp distinction between gospel content and teaching as there is a vital dependent relationship.

---

[28] C. H. Dodd, *The Apostolic Preaching and Its Development* (New York: Willett, Clark & Co., 1937), p. 8.

It is helpful to visualize the New Testament materials as forming three concentric circles around the death, resurrection, and exaltation of Christ. The first circle is the *kerygma*, which interprets these events with a view to bringing men to faith in Christ. The second circle is the theological expansion of the first. Its purpose is to lead the new believer into a fuller apprehension of what God has accomplished through Christ Jesus. The outside circle is the ethical expansion of the other two. It lays hold on this new relationship of man to God and brings it into focus for practical daily living.[29]

The content or message of the Christian gospel merged with the fervent moral addresses of the Hebrew prophets. In the first three centuries following Christ the uniting of the rhetorical stream and the Hebrew-Christian streams was completed. From these three historical foundations Christian preaching originated. The development of Christian preaching may be divided into eight periods.

Development of Christian Preaching

The ancient period.—From A.D. 70 to A.D. 430 has been designated as the ancient or Patristic period for preaching.[30] Within this broad expanse of time two clearly marked periods are discernible: A.D. 70 to 300 and A.D. 300 to 430.

The period A.D. 70-300 was a time of great crises. The fall of Jerusalem, the expansion of the Roman Empire, and the persecutions of the Christians profoundly influenced preaching during this period.

For about one hundred years following the death of Peter and Paul, *ca.* 70 to 170, traces of preaching are very rare, and these do not reveal any great power. Near the end of the second century in the work of Origen, Clement of Alexandria, Irenaeus, and Hippolytus there is clear evidence of an increase in the power of preaching.

Flexibility and informality characterized early preaching. The

---

[29] Mounce, *op. cit.*, p. 133.
[30] Dargan, *A History of Preaching*, I, 28.

early conception was that anyone could preach, and men spoke
as God moved them. Later the idea developed that preaching
should be confined to an official class. When the preacher spoke,
he would usually sit and address the people. Occasionally a
preacher would write out and read his sermon, but in general
sermon preparation and delivery were very formal. Three
sources supplied content for the preachers: (1) apostolic tradition, (2) the Bible, (3) the preachers' own personal contributions. In form the sermon was the homily, or unpretentious
address, or simply a running comment on Scripture.

Preaching of the early Patristic period had less spiritual power
than that of the apostolic period, and it was more impersonal as
time separated the minister from Christ. Preaching was also
quite unstable as preachers waxed hot and cold.

On the positive side, preaching was successful because of the
natural power of the gospel. In addition, several external factors
aided Christianity: the Roman world was at peace; communication lines were open; old Greco-Roman religions were disinte-
grating; the preachers were faithful to their task of preaching;
they were free from professionalism; and their preaching was
personal, simple, and direct.

Three classifications of preachers have been set out by
Dargan.[31] The Apostolic Fathers, so called because they were
supposed to have been disciples of the original apostles, were
Ignatius, Polycarp, Clement of Rome, and an unknown Clement of the second century. Other men, called Apologists, de-
fended the faith by writing and pleading with secular authorities
for fair treatment for Christianity. Dionysius, Justin Martyr,
Tatian, and Tertullian were among the best known of this
group. Several men won distinction as theologians (Ante-Nicene
group) and are usually classified as such. In the East Origen,
Clement of Alexandria, Gregory Thaumaturgus, Dorotheus,
Lucian, Diodorus, and Theodore were the primary leaders. In
the West the leaders were Irenaeus, Hippolytus, Tertullian, and
Cyprian.

[31] *Ibid.*, chapter I.

The period A.D. 300 to 430 saw a remarkable rise in the power of preaching. This is one of five climactic periods in the history of Christian preaching. Governmental help and blessing, social prestige, the people's love for oratory, education, and excellent schools played prominent roles in advancing preaching to new heights. Within Christianity, more forms in sermons, a closed canon, more biblical preaching, a more orderly worship service, stability of doctrines, and the culture and training of preachers added luster to the pulpit. The great preachers during this period were Basil the Great, Gregory Nazianzen, Gregory of Nyssa, Chrysostom, Hilary, Ambrose, and Augustine.

The Dark Ages.—The years from A.D. 430 to 1095 saw the power of the pulpit all but destroyed as a long black night of ignorance settled over the so-called "civilized world." Preaching suffered along with all religious and social institutions. Preachers were corrupt; the liturgy strangled the power of the pulpit; the sacerdotal spirit grew until the preacher became the priest. Doctrinal controversies became common in the face of mounting corruption of doctrine. From without, hordes of barbarians came storming into the Christian world. Fanaticism and superstition abounded; the worship of angels, saints, relics, and Mary replaced the worship of Christ. Preachers were ignorant and drunk on perverted allegory.

Here and there a man held high a better conception of Christianity. Men such as Bede, Patrick, Gall, Boniface, and Eligius attempted to understand the Word of God and to propagate the message of salvation as they understood it. These years as a whole were the lowest, darkest, and most corrupt in the history of preaching.

The scholastic age.—The time from 1095 to 1361 has been called the scholastic age. Four forces helped to awaken Europe, the church, and preaching during these years. Scholasticism ushered in a new concern for learning. The Crusades under the leadership of men such as Peter the Hermit and Pope Urban II brought Europe into touch with the culture and commerce of the Orient and thereby quickened the pulse of the peoples of

the West. Mysticism developed and brought a fresh breath of
spiritual power to a decadent religion. During this time the mis-
sionary preaching orders developed. Driven by a genuine love
for people, Francis of Assisi began a movement for taking Christianity to people in need; from his zeal sprang the Franciscans.
About the same time Dominic, concerned for the welfare of the
Catholic Church, initiated a movement to convert heretics and
conserve the weak in faith. Because these men did so much effective preaching, this period, especially the latter part, is known
as a revival period in the history of Christian pulpit.

The reformatory age.—The period from 1361 to 1572 has
been designated as the reformatory age. Usually the preachers
of this period have been listed as prereformers (1361 to 1500)
and reformers (1500 to 1572).

In the pre-Reformation period preaching declined. Popular,
scholastic, and mystical were the typical descriptions of preachers. A few men of power dared to raise their voices and cry for
better days. The ministries of John Wycliffe, John Huss, and
Savonarola were most instrumental in preparing for the Reformation.

The Reformation itself brought a genuine revival in preaching as the leaders made the preaching of the Word central in
their task. After a thousand years of being relegated to a secondary role behind the Mass, preaching emerged as the most
effective method for proclaiming God's good news. Luther,
Calvin, Zwingli, Latimer, Knox, and a great host of others broke
the shackles that had bound preaching and liberated God's
chosen means for telling the world about his Son and salvation.
These men were not merely preachers, but they were biblical
preachers. The pulpit was central; the sermon was in the language of the people; and the Bible was the supreme authority for
the spoken messages. The reformers recognized, practiced, and
taught that preaching was the primary function of a minister of
the Lord Jesus Christ.

The seventeenth century.—The years from 1572 to 1700 have
been called the fifth period in the history of preaching. Through-

out most of the Christian world preaching declined following
the Reformation. Such was not the case in France and England
where these years are known as the "classic age of preaching."

In France King Louis XIV led his people to great advances
in material prosperity and in intellectual development. He loved
preaching and made it popular and socially acceptable. In 1598
the Edict of Nantes provided religious toleration and thereby
stimulated both Protestants and Catholics to greater efforts. This
was the period of the great Catholic preachers: Bossuet, Bourda-
loue, Fenelon, and Massillon.

In England in 1611 the King James Version of the Bible was
published and initiated its era of influence and dominance that
has lasted until this day. The seventeenth century was great in
literary output but poor in morality. The English preachers were
motivated to great efforts to correct these abuses. Among the
great preachers were Richard Baxter, John Bunyan, Jeremy
Taylor, and John Donne.

The eighteenth century.—The eighteenth century was the
century of John and Charles Wesley and George Whitefield.
Their work constituted the high point in a century of low
morals, poor preaching, a weak church, and spineless doctrine.
They were leaders of the evangelical revival in England and
the Great Awakening in America.

The evangelical revival, in all probability, saved England
from the moral destruction which befell France during the same
century. In America the Great Awakening was responsible for a
renewed vitality of American church life. Theodore Frelinghuy-
sen, Gilbert Tennent, Jonathan Edwards, and George Whitefield led this great movement.

The nineteenth century.—The nineteenth century was one of
the mountain peaks in the march of man through the ages.
Great ideas and movements shaped the preaching of these days.
Democracy, industry, science, reform, slavery, education, eco-
nomics, missions, and church organizations are terms which
characterize the century.

Great men dominated the preaching of this century. Charles

G. Finney, Horace Bushnell, Henry Ward Beecher, Phillips
Brooks, John A. Broadus, Thomas de Witt Talmage, Dwight
L. Moody, Thomas Chalmers, F. W. Robertson, Charles Haddon Spurgeon, Alexander Maclaren, and Joseph Parker stand
among the mighty pulpit giants of the ages. Preaching reached
one of its climactic periods of development during these years.
God raised up men of ability who understood their task as
preachers. These men preached with clarity, vividness, and
power. In the strength of the pulpit this century can be compared to the first century with Peter and Paul and to the fourth
century with Chrysostom and Augustine.

The twentieth century.—The twentieth century was ushered
in with emphasis on the social aspects of Christianity. Walter
Rauschenbusch was the prophet of the new order. Many perver-
sions and corruptions came into the pulpit through a misunderstanding of what the gospel really was. While the preachers in
the first century fully understood that the *kerygma* came first
and then the *didaché*, men in the early days of the twentieth
century did not. Gradually, in this century, progress has been
made in securing a balance between gospel and ethical development.

Though it is much too early to produce an objective evalua-
tion of the status of preaching in this century, it is evident that
there has been a significant content drought in modern preaching. The unparallelled growth of churches and the demands of
a materialistic society have forced ministers to relegate study
and sermon preparation to a secondary role while the roles of
administrator, pastor, organizer, counselor, and teacher supersede
that of preacher.

Whenever Christianity has made substantial progress, great
preaching has led the way. In the history of Christianity there
have been five great centuries of growth and development.
These same five periods are the five centuries of great preaching:
the first with the apostles, the fourth with Chrysostom and
Augustine, the thirteenth with Francis of Assisi and Dominic,
the sixteenth with Luther and Calvin, and the nineteenth with

Spurgeon and Maclaren. Contrariwise, whenever preaching has declined, Christianity has become stagnant. In the Dark Ages, in the fourteenth and fifteenth centuries, and in the seventeenth and eighteenth centuries, in most countries preaching was weak and ineffective.

God ordained preaching to proclaim his message to all mankind. When preachers have failed to understand God's method and message, God's kingdom has been hindered. When men heard God call, understood their task, and faithfully delivered his message, the kingdom has moved forward for his glory.

II

Discovering the Idea
of the Sermon

The beginning of a sermon is the conception of the idea of
the message in the mind and heart of the preacher. The time of
this conception is often lost in mystery. It may take place at
almost any moment and often quite apart from any conscious
effort on the part of the preacher.

By the idea of the sermon is meant an insight into a truth as it
relates to life experience. It is the germinal truth of the sermon,
the thought from which the sermon emerges and develops. As
such it is the central truth of the sermon, a truth which consti-
tutes its starting point and is its bond of unity.

Sources of the Idea of the Sermon

The idea of the sermon may emerge from several sources:
the experience of the people, the Scriptures, a planned program
of preaching, the experience of the preacher, and flashes of
inspiration.

The Experience of the People

*"Concrete human problems, and the Gospel answer, is the
best starting-place for sermons."* [1] Preaching is designed to meet
human need. The objectives of preaching previously defined
indicate that this is true.[2] As the preacher sees his people and
understands their needs, ideas which should be discussed will
emerge.

[1] Samuel M. Shoemaker, *The Church Alive* (New York: E. P. Dutton &
Co., 1950), p. 63.
[2] See pp. 15-18.

30

The preacher must know the needs of his people.—To meet
human needs in preaching the preacher must know the needs of
his people. He must have a knowledge of human nature. That
is, he must know the timeless questions of men. Across the centuries men have asked and sought answers to the same questions.
Often they are phrased in different ways and are asked in different contexts, but they are essentially the same. They are questions about eternal realities. Is there a God? What is he like?
Can man know him and have fellowship with him? Is there life
beyond this life? If so, what is it like? Will man share in its
values? What is death and what is its significance? What is life?
Is it worthwhile? What about sorrow and tragedy? Why should
evil even have existed? What about the sense of guilt and the
fact of sin? How can man escape their power? Is there any for-
giveness, accompanied by ease of conscience? Why should life
with its crises and its daily routine be so frustrating? Is there any
hope for victory over the frustrations of life? These questions,
with countless others, have been asked by men the world over
and through all ages. As timeless and universal questions they
must be taken into consideration in preaching.

The preacher must have a knowledge of the times in which
his people live. This is more than to say that he must know what
is happening in his congregation. Too often preachers are handi-
capped by provincialism in their knowledge of their times. They
see life in terms of the more immediate eddies without realizing
that there are great currents of world life and thought of which
the provincial circumstances are only a small and sometimes
relatively insignificant fragment. There needs to be a knowledge
of the broad sweep of history and life of which a particular person is a part.

But the preacher must also know a particular church and its
people. He can easily be perplexed and lost in the great sweep of
world movements. He needs to know particular men and women
with their specific needs.

He needs knowledge of the common affairs and the crisis
experiences of individual lives. He needs to know life's trage-

dies, the disappointments and heartaches that people bear. He
needs to know life's triumphs, the small but significant hours
of victory in the lives of people. There is the hour of the marriage ceremony, the birth of a child into the family, the first day
at school, graduation, the first job, a promotion. The preacher
needs to know life's significant and critical moments and periods:
adolescence, the step from youth to manhood or womanhood,
"the middle time of life," and old age.

The preacher can know the needs of his people.—An understanding of people begins first of all in the preacher's understanding of himself. He needs to see himself first in relation to
these great areas and influences of human experience. Seeing
himself thus, he must understand himself in relation to them.
In other words, he must through the help of Christ achieve
victory in life. He must be capable of seeing himself and his life
objectively. It is only as he has objective appraisal of himself
that he can be certain that he sees and understands people as they
really are.

To understand people the preacher must cultivate the pastoral
heart—sympathy and compassion for people. In one sense the
pastoral heart either exists in a man or it doesn't. It is doubtful
that God would call a man into the ministry in whom it does
not inherently or potentially exist. Yet the pastoral heart is subject to development through nurture and cultivation. George
W. Truett has said, "I have sought the pastoral heart." When
the preacher loves people and observes them with sympathy, his
understanding of them grows.

To understand people the preacher must move among them in
a faithful ministry. While he will not mechanically look for
knowledge of his people, he will keep his eyes open. He will
observe how people live, think, and seem to feel. He will listen
to people, and by listening he will learn much. People will discuss their problems and lay bare their souls to the faithful pastor.
He will ask questions, discreet and discerning questions, designed
to cultivate understanding. The people will make suggestions.
They will express their ideas. In his work as a pastor the preacher

will have opportunity to counsel people. When they are assured that what they tell is held in strictest confidence, people will open their hearts and lives to him. Their sins, doubts, fears, frustrations, and ambitions will be laid before him.

The preacher should share in the life experiences of his people. He should share their hours of tragedy and their hours of triumph. He must live with them. In doing so he comes to understand them by seeing life through their eyes and experience.

The pastor can understand the times in which his people live through a study of history; through analysis of the age of which his particular generation is a part. He may read philosophy and world thought until he feels that he has a grasp of what is happening in his world. Only as he sees his people in this context can he really understand them.

A careful survey of the pastor's community will reveal significant facts. Many pastors have made such studies and have developed their preaching and activities in the light of their findings. The preacher can utilize the results of the religious census. It is interesting what the discerning pastor can see in the information on a census card. He could use a committee to study the needs of his field, or he might use, as some churches have, a counseling group. One church used such a committee made up of a lawyer, a doctor, a psychologist, a housewife, and an effective personal evangelist. The results and the information of such activity can be continually passed along to the pastor.

When the preacher thus knows people, the possibilities for preaching become numberless. Sermon ideas are everywhere in the lives and experiences of his people. The preacher needs only to keep his homiletical eye open to see what has been and is always there. Henry Sloane Coffin has said: "The most useful sermons came to me as a pastor in visiting in the homes of my congregation, or from other contacts with individuals. Their questions or their situations clutched at my heart, and I turned to the Word of God in the Scriptures for an answer." [3]

---

[3] "The Interpreter's Discipline," in *Here Is My Method*, ed. Donald Macleod (Westwood, N.J.: Fleming H. Revell Co., 1952), p. 59.

The Scriptures

The Bible is the record of God's progressive revelation of himself to men. It is the story of God's confrontation of men in the actual experiences of life. God met men in the tragedies, the crises, the triumphs, the aspirations of life, and in so doing made himself known to them. Because its pages were wrought out in actual experiences, the Bible has a message for life. The God who made himself known to men in past experiences is available to men today. The Bible as the message of life experience with God is eternally contemporary. Its stories and its messages are always relevant. The Bible meets men today where they have real need, just as the God of the Bible met men yesterday in their needs.

The text as a scriptural fabric of the sermon.—The term "text" is derived from the Latin *textus*, which in turn came from the verb *texere* meaning to weave, to construct, to compose. *Textus* is the product of the weaving, texture, web, structure. Text is thus the fabric of one's thinking expressed orally or in writing. As applied to preaching, the text was formally regarded as the scriptural fabric of the sermon into which were woven the comments and interpretations of the preacher.[4] As preaching developed, the text became shorter, and the comments and interpretation became longer until the text became simply a scriptural starting point or foundation of the sermon.

Correctly defined, the text is the scriptural fabric or structure of the sermon. Into this fabric the preacher weaves his interpretation, illustrations, and applications to produce the sermon.

The methods of finding texts.—The discovery of the text is one of the preacher's most interesting and significant tasks. Its discovery may come in one of two ways. The text may find the preacher or the searching preacher may find the text.

Often in the preacher's own devotional reading of the Scripture a passage will grip his heart and stimulate his mind. The text will literally beg to be preached.

[4] See John A. Broadus, *On the Preparation and Delivery of Sermons.* Rev. ed. by Jesse B. Weatherspoon (New York: Harper & Bros., 1944).

Sometimes the text finds him [the preacher]—leaps up at him out of the page, demanding to be used and made known in all of the riches of its truth. These are the happiest moments of a preacher's life, for he goes to his task with joy that he has the right word.[5]

That passage which has gripped the preacher will have a vitality about it when used as the scriptural fabric of a message that hardly any other passage can have.

The devotional method of finding a text is not the usual method of text discovery. More often the preacher will find texts because he is searching for them. He may already have a sermon idea from the needs of the people. His search then will be for a text that will help him to unfold and relate the idea to the revelation of God and to the lives of the people. Or he may be searching for a passage of Scripture that will have life interest for his people today, and out of it may develop a topic. Regardless of the approach, the discovery of the text is often the result of a quest.

The principles for the search for texts.—In the search for a text certain principles should be observed. The preacher should take into consideration the congregation for whom the sermon is prepared. Attention must be given to their needs. But attention also must be given to the intellectual and spiritual capacities of the congregation. Some congregations are spiritually immature and undeveloped. They are not prepared for the weightier matters of Scripture. The texts and the truths involved in sermons preached to them must be relatively simple and easily understood. Other congregations are characterized by spiritual maturity and the capacity for serious thinking. For them, passages could be chosen that would lead to discussion of the more serious and difficult truths of the Christian faith.

The text should usually be a complete unit of thought. To isolate a word, phrase, or clause from its context as the basis for a sermon is doubtful procedure. The same may be said for the

---

[5] Willard Brewing, "The Sermon I Might Have Preached, If!" in Macleod *op. cit.*, p. 38.

isolation of a verse of Scripture from its context. The text should be selected in connection with its context.

Texts should be clear and simple—texts that rather readily reveal their meaning. If not, then they should be capable of clear and easy exposition. The more difficult passages have their place in the sermon but are better used in some way other than as the scriptural fabric of the sermon. A simple text is characterized by positive affirmation of the truth expressed in plain language.

Usually the preacher should select texts that are familiar and well-loved. Some texts have been used in all generations of Christian preaching and are well known to most Christians. For this reason, preachers avoid them. They suppose, for one thing, that they need not be preached. They also recognize the difficulty of saying something new and fresh about such a text. Yet such familiar passages as John 3:16, Romans 1:16, 1 Corinthians 13, John 14:1-6, and Matthew 5:1-12 offer endless resources for sermons. They are great and good texts. This explains why they have been often used and have endured. The very familiarity of people with them gives them added value. A veritable treasure of associations is clustered about these texts in the memory of the people. The use of the familiar text will draw such associations into active consciousness, giving added blessing to the hearers. Someone has said, "Familiar texts are the jewels of the pulpit; diamonds are never obsolete."

The preacher should occasionally select new or novel texts—novel, different, and unusual but not sensational. Two of Horace Bushnell's sermons illustrate this principle. His sermon on "Every Man's Life a Plan of God" is based on Isaiah 45:5. Speaking of Cyrus, God said, "I am the Lord, and there is none else, there is no God beside me: I girded thee, though thou hast not known me." Bushnell's sermon is based on the latter part of this verse: *I will gird thee, though thou hast not known me.* In Bushnell's day this was a new and unusual text by which to develop the idea that every man's life is directed of the Lord. The novelty of the text is one reason why the sermon has endured as a great pulpit masterpiece.

His other well-known sermon is entitled, "Unconscious Influence." Its text is John 20:8. "Then went in also that other disciple." Peter and the beloved disciple had run to the tomb on the resurrection morning. The other disciple had arrived first and waited outside until Peter, arriving at the tomb, immediately went in. Then the other followed him. "Thus it is that men are ever touching unconsciously the springs of motion in each other; thus it is that one man, without thought or intention, or even a consciousness of the fact, is ever leading some other after him." [6]

Thus in a simple historical statement Bushnell found a significant and stimulating truth. This was a new and different way of getting at an old truth. The very newness of the approach makes the sermon attractive and impressive.

The preacher's selection of texts should be varied. It should be varied at least in the sense that he selects them from all portions of the Scriptures. There is a common tendency among preachers to neglect portions of Scripture. Some habitually preach from the New Testament and neglect the Old Testament. Others, greatly interested in the types and figures of the Old Testament, neglect the New Testament. Other preachers become interested in doctrinal hobbies and, in preaching on their favorite themes, neglect other great themes and segments of Scripture.

The habit of neglecting portions of Scripture can be avoided by following a regularly planned program of preaching. Such a program should take into account the necessity of preaching on all portions of Scripture.

A Planned Program of Preaching

In a planned program of preaching the preacher chooses in advance his topics, text, and objectives for sermons for a given period of time. Some advocate that the preacher should plan for a year in advance; this is possible and has been done. It is more likely, however, that the average preacher would prefer plan-

---

[6] "Unconscious Influence," in *The World's Great Sermons*, comp. Grenville Kleiser (New York: Funk & Wagnalls Co., 1908), IV, 235.

ning for a shorter period of time. He might work on the basis of three months or experiment with planning for even one month.

The need for a planned program of preaching.—The need for such a program may be seen in its advantages. It enables the preacher to know well in advance what he is going to preach. It reduces the tense emotional struggle involved in the selecting of topics week by week. It enables the preacher to conserve both time and energy. It gives the preacher more time to think about his sermons and to study for them. It gives the topic opportunity to grow in his own mind. It gives more time for research and the gathering of material. Other factors being equal, the best sermon is the product of diligent and careful study.

A planned program of preaching insures a better balance in the preacher's topics and texts. Based on a study and knowledge of the needs of the people, the program will be designed to meet all of these needs. Thus there will be a better balance in the treatment of the needs of the people. Such a program will give due attention to all the significant themes of the Scriptures, thus assuring a more balanced diet of biblical preaching.

A planned program of preaching will give better opportunity for conducting the worship service around the theme of the sermon. In those churches where the sermon is the central act of worship, the idea of the sermon and its place in the service of worship are important. With his theme in hand, the preacher himself can help to plan the worship service, or he can more effectively advise those who will plan it.

The factors to be considered in planning for preaching.—In planning for a program of preaching many factors must be taken into consideration. Attention should be given to the general situation and the specific needs of the church. The intellectual and spiritual capacity of the people must be considered. Their problems and burdens must be taken into account. The circumstances under which they live must be noted. The preacher must ask and attempt to answer with a discerning pastoral heart, "What are the needs of people to which I must address myself?"

The program of activity of the local church must be considered, both the annual features and the special occasions. There are revivals to be conducted, mission offerings to be taken, stewardship campaigns to be promoted, and a multitude of other things to be accomplished. An effective preaching program must take account of and be geared into this program.

The denominational calendar of activity will also influence sermon themes. Most churches participate in the varied activities sponsored by the denomination, and these things will affect the type of sermon which a man will want to preach.

There are special days and weeks to be considered. Some groups observe the Christian year faithfully, and this practice definitely determines many themes and Scripture passages for the preacher. For those who do not observe the Christian year there are special days to which attention might well be given. Some preachers take note of and preach special sermons on Christmas, Thanksgiving, Easter, New Year's Day, Mother's Day, Labor Day, and Father's Day. Each preacher within his own faith, will have to determine those seasons which seem to be worthy of his attention.

Emphases in Bible study in Sunday school and themes in training organizations should be taken into account. The preacher may wish to supplement the program of Bible study in the Sunday school, or he may wish to preach from entirely different types of passages from those used in the Bible study. Thus, if the lessons were in the New Testament historical material, he might wish to preach from the Old Testament prophetic literature.

Community and world situations will also affect sermon plans. The preacher should consider varied factors in working out his program. Everything that he knows or anticipates about his congregation and community and the gospel's relation to these things should be considered.

A method for developing a planned preaching program.—The method of developing a planned program of preaching will vary with each minister, according to his temperament and disposition, but a suggested one is presented here. In evaluating his congregation's needs, the preacher will try to determine what objectives are of primary concern. They have been previously listed and defined [7] as evangelistic, consecrative, doctrinal, ethical, devotional, and pastoral (comforting). One pastor may determine that his opportunity and needs are mainly evangelistic, arriving at the conclusion that at least half of his sermons should be evangelistic. Another pastor may decide that the greatest need is for the growth of his people in Christian character and service because his evangelistic opportunities are limited. He may plan to preach more didactic (doctrinal and ethical) and consecrative sermons. Every church has distinctive needs, hence the emphases or objectives may vary greatly.

Having determined the objectives for his preaching, the preacher should then list the special days that he intends to emphasize in his program. He should list the emphases of his local church and of the denomination that call for attention. After thinking and praying about this program with these several factors in mind, he should then set himself to the preparation of the program.

It is suggested that he use one sheet of paper for each service, dating these sheets for one month in advance. On each sheet of paper, in connection with each service, he should list any special days and local church or denominational emphases. Having done this for each service, he should go over them, and in the light of the needs of his church, the days to be emphasized, the local church and denominational programs to be emphasized, assign major objectives to sermons for each service.

With a balanced program of Bible preaching in mind he should assign to each service a sermon idea and a text. All of this would be subject to further refinement, restatement, and revision.

Working out such a program will take time; it will also take careful thought and prayerful devotion. Yet out of such careful preparation can come a well-balanced, purposeful, and spiritual-

[7] See pp. 15-18.

ly guided program of preaching. Occasional emergencies may force the preacher to turn away from the planned program, and he should not hesitate to do so when necessary, returning to his plan as soon as possible.

The Preacher's Own Experience

The idea of the sermon will often come from the preacher's own personal experience. Sermon ideas will be found in his own spiritual crises: his conversion, his call to the ministry, his experience with tragedy and sorrow, his triumphs in Christ. They will develop from his understanding of his own spiritual needs. Those things which he understands as the needs of his own soul are often the needs of other souls. To discuss his own spiritual needs will be to discuss the needs of others.

Sermon ideas are discovered by the preacher as he shares in the spiritual experiences of others. He sees and helps others to find victory over sin, doubt, fear. Without revealing secrets learned in confidence, he can help others through sermon ideas growing out of his counseling experiences.

The preacher will discover preaching ideas in his reading and in listening to the sermons of other men. Although he will not borrow and preach sermons or sermon outlines of others, his own thinking will be stimulated by them, and ideas will come as he reads or as he listens to another preacher.

Preaching ideas will emerge from the minister's conception of his task as a prophet, teacher, pastor, or counselor. As he sees himself as a prophet, he will feel that he must speak to the public issues of his day. As a teacher he must teach the great fundamentals of the faith. He is a pastor and must meet the needs of his people. He is a counselor and must discuss the basic concerns of those to whom he ministers.

Flashes of Inspiration

Sometimes the idea for a sermon comes as a flash of inspiration, for which there seems to have been no previous preparation.

The beginning of a sermon with me is that moment when a spark is struck by the steel of the Word in the Bible on the flint of some human need. The spark is an idea, a fresh insight, a heightened emotional and intellectual response to a verse or passage of scripture . . . or the flash of the Gospel's answer to some troubling human problem.[8]

This flash of inspiration may come at any time and under almost any kind of circumstance. It may be the result of the workings of the preacher's subconscious mind. It may be by the leadership of the Holy Spirit. Often these ideas are the best that the preacher ever discovers—more correctly, that discover him. Usually these flashes are illusory and short-lived. For this reason it is wise to record them when they occur. The preacher should carry a notebook or note cards for such flashes of insight. Thus, he will conserve for himself more than just the pleasant feeling that he has discovered a stimulating idea. Making the note will also start some subconscious consideration of the idea.

Stabilizing the Idea of the Sermon

The idea of the sermon at this point is only an insight, a thought in germinal form that has potential for sermon development. It is necessary to formulate, to develop, and to relate the idea to a text, a thesis, and a specific objective.

Relating the Idea to a Text

The idea for the sermon may begin in several places other than in Scripture. When the idea does start in a (1) congregational need, (2) in a planned program, (3) in the preacher's personal life, or (4) in a flash of insight, the sermon builder should secure a text to match. By following suggestions set out earlier in this chapter the minister should be able to do this in a satisfactory way. Of course, if the idea is born in Scripture, the text will have been chosen. Chapter 3 will discuss the interpretation of this text.

---

[8] Eugene Carson Blake, "Flint Strikes Steel," in Macleod, *op. cit.*, p. 25.

Relating the Idea to the Thesis

The thesis (proposition) of the sermon is the statement in a brief declarative sentence of the central idea of the message. The thesis is the gist of the sermon in a sentence. It has sometimes been identified with the theme of the sermon. It has also been designated as the "key sentence" of the sermon. J. H. Jowett has said, "No sermon is ready for preaching, not ready for writing out, until we can express its theme in a short, pregnant sentence as clear as a crystal." [9] Such a sentence is the thesis.

Some theses gleaned from the preaching of Robert South read as follows: "Religion is the best reason of state"; "Good intentions are no excuse for bad actions"; "Concealment of sin is no security to the sinner"; "The instruments which God chooses are not such as man would have chosen."

A sermon on regeneration or the necessity of the new birth, based on the third chapter of John's Gospel, might have the following thesis: "Regardless of background and culture man needs a transforming experience of renewal wrought by the Holy Spirit." A sermon on the topic, "A New Day and a New Life," could have as its thesis, "You can begin life over again in the Lord." A sermon on the topic, "Through Failure to Victory," may have as its thesis, "Our failures can be used as steppingstones to victory."

In Fosdick's sermon, "Christians in Spite of Everything," there is this sentence: "Christianity essentially means a spiritual victory in the face of hostile circumstances." [10] This is the thesis, the central truth of this sermon. In his sermon, "Escape from Frustration," [11] James Reid says, "The way out of life's frustrations is found, not by resenting our limitations, but by accepting the place of frustration as the sphere of God's purpose." In each instance the central idea of the sermon, its thesis, has been cast into a brief, germinal, declarative sentence.

---

[9] J. H. Jowett, *The Preacher: His Life and Work* (New York: George H. Doran Co., 1912), p. 133.

[10] Broadus, *On the Preparation and Delivery of Sermons*, p. 56.

[11] *Ibid.*

A good thesis or proposition should be brief, concise. It should contain no unnecessary words. Every word should be essential to its meaning. Ordinarily a good thesis is stated in no more than eight to fifteen words.

A good thesis should be characterized by human interest. To create human interest the thesis should be personal in the sense that it touches the mood and manner of speech of those who will see or hear it. It should be in touch with life as people live it. It should touch the basic and fundamental questions that men ask and should relate to the basic experiences of life.

A good thesis is fresh and attractive. It should be characterized by vitality and difference. This, plus the fact that it is briefly and concisely stated, gives to it something of the quality of an adage or maxim. It is almost proverbial in force.

A good thesis is timeless and universal. It should be in touch with life and is therefore timely. But it should also be stated in the form of a truth that is good for all time. It should contain no historical references, such as personalities, places, or events.

Writing out a thesis is an interesting and creative task. Begin by studying the text and the idea of the sermon with a view of stating the central truth in one sentence. In doing so, write out more than one statement of the thesis. In this first writing make no particular effort at a condensation or final statement. Then write and rewrite the proposition. Change words or phrases, cut out unnecessary words, add essential words, exchange large words for small words, use concrete rather than abstract terms.

Relating the Idea to the Objective

The idea of the sermon should be related to the objective of the sermon. As defined in chapter 1,[12] the objective has three dimensions: total, major, specific. After the preacher has secured his idea and related it to a text and a thesis, he should write out his *purpose*. The purpose of a sermon should be to meet some basic need in the lives of the people.

[12] See pp. 15-18.

Donald Miller defines aim in preaching by saying: "The aim consists in what we desire that truth [the theme of the sermon] to do to the hearer, or what we desire the hearer to do in response to the truth." [13] It is not enough merely to state the truth clearly. Theological truth always has an end in view in the lives of people. The preacher should study the needs of his people and the relation of the truths of his passage to these needs. The true aim of a sermon is what the preacher desires to happen in the experience of the hearers in response to its truth.

By the same process in which he developed the thesis he should formulate and write out the specific objective of his sermon. The specific objective should be written with a strong verb calling for action on the part of the people. A specific objective can best be understood when seen in connection with the topic, the text, and the proposition.

Topic:	"Is Drinking a Religious Problem?"
Text:	Isaiah 5:11-16, 20-23
Proposition:	The expanding liquor traffic presents a challenge . . . [to] Christian men and women.[14]
Specific Objective:[15]	That Christian men and women resist unconditionally the liquor traffic.
Topic:	"Pagans Have No Hope"
Text:	Ephesians 2:11-12
Proposition:	The triumphant message of Christmas is the hope which it gives to the world.[16]
Specific Objective:	That Christian people provide the gospel for the pagan world.
Topic:	"Six Days for Labor"
Text:	Exodus 20:9

---

[13] *The Way to Biblical Preaching*, p. 114.

[14] Harold A. Bosley, "Is Drinking a Religious Problem?" *Pulpit Digest*, XXXIII (October, 1952), 27.

[15] These specific objectives are supplied by the authors of this book.

[16] Gerald Kennedy, "Pagans Have No Hope," *Pulpit Digest*, XXXIII (December, 1952), 21.

Proposition:	The preservation of our way of life depends upon a return to worship by the working man.[17]
Specific Objective:	The desired result for this message is that working men and women worship regularly and effectively.
Topic:	"How You Can Fashion Your Future"
Text:	Genesis 39
Proposition:	Faith in God is the best foundation for our lives.[18]
Specific Objective:	The goal for this sermon is that the people prepare for the future by by having a vital faith in God.
Topic:	"The Church's Commission in Our Day"
Text:	Isaiah 6:8-9a
Proposition:	The hope for our world lives in the translation of our faith into action.[19]
Specific Objective:	The desired result of this message is that Christians witness to the world through their living faith.

Stating an aim in this manner will enable the preacher to concentrate his preparation. Having a specific objective will help him focus all his thoughts and force in the sermon toward achieving the desired result.

The thesis of the sermon is the central idea or truth to be presented in the message. The specific objective is the desired impact of this truth in the lives of the hearers. To formulate both carefully and precisely is a strategically important step in sermon preparation.

---

[17] William P. Vaughn, "Six Days for Labor," *Pulpit Digest,* XXXV (August, 1955), 20.

[18] Denver Jackson Davis, "How You Can Fashion Your Future," *Pulpit Digest,* XXXV (June, 1955), 35.

[19] Samuel M. Shoemaker, "The Church's Commission in Our Day," *Pulpit Digest,* XXXV (May, 1955), 41.

III

Interpreting the Text

"To interpret and apply his text in accordance with its real meaning is one of the preacher's most sacred duties."[1] This is true because Scripture is the revealed truth of God given to man for the purpose of redemption. Serious and eternal issues are involved in the proclamation of this truth. Lives of men today and eternal destiny tomorrow depend upon accurate and effective interpretation of the truth of God as revealed in Scripture. Such a task cannot be done without the Spirit's aid.

The history of interpretation has been long and varied. A brief study of the different approaches to interpretation will both warn of pitfalls to be avoided and commend worthy examples to be followed.

The Methods of Interpretation

Allegorical Interpretation

One of the earliest approaches to the understanding of the Bible, allegorical interpretation is the search for those truths in a passage of Scripture which are metaphorically implied but not expressly stated. The literal sense of the passage is regarded as the vehicle for portraying more profound spiritual meaning.

The allegorical method had its origin in Greek philosophy as early as the sixth century B.C. The advance of Greek philosophy brought the rejection of Homer and the other ancient writings of Greece. In order to meet the advance of Greek philosophy, the religionists of the day adopted the method of allegory to discover hidden and deeper meanings in the ancient writings.

[1] Broadus, *On the Preparation and Delivery of Sermons,* p. 24.

This method was transferred to Jewish interpretation by the conflict of the Jewish Scriptures with Greek philosophy. Philo was the first to attempt to harmonize the two by allegorizing. According to Philo, Scripture had both a literal and an allegorical meaning. By finding hidden meanings in Scripture, he was able to reconcile the ideas and institutions of Judaism with Hellenistic culture. For example, Philo made the four rivers of Eden represent the virtues of prudence, temperance, courage, and justice. The main stream from which they branch is goodness, the basic virtue of life.

Allegorical interpretation was developed in Christian circles by the school of Pantaenus (A.D. 180) in Alexandria. The two pre-eminent representatives of this school were Clement of Alexandria and Origen. Clement contended that Scripture had three meanings: the literal, the moral, and the spiritual. The spiritual was considered the highest meaning. The literal meaning furnished only an elementary faith while the spiritual sense led to true knowledge. In interpreting the story of the prodigal son, the robe which the father called for to be put on the son was immortality; the shoes represented the upward progress of the soul; and the fatted calf was Christ. Thus, even incidental factors are given sublime significance.

Origen also believed that Scripture had a literal, moral, and spiritual significance. In interpreting John 1:27, "the latchet of whose shoes I am not worthy to unloose," Origen said that this referred to the fact that few can understand the mystery of Christ's incarnation. The plural "shoes" represented the incarnation and descent into Hades. Both of these are mysteries difficult to comprehend.

Allegorical interpretation has been practiced in Christian circles since Origen as a method of interpretation. Broadus says that "a good and safe rule to follow is that, while probable allegorical or spiritual meanings may be adduced as probable, no allegorical meaning shall be made the basis of a sermon without clear warrant in Scripture usage." [2]

_____
[2] *On the Preparation and Delivery of Sermons*, p. 34.

Dogmatic Interpretation

Dogmatic interpretation is the approach to Scripture in which creedal orthodoxy is viewed "as the governing principle of all exegetical effort." [3] Dana and Glaze describe dogmatic exegesis as exhibiting the following process: "Influential Church leaders thought out and promulgated certain theories regarding the Christian religion; these theories were then read into the Scriptures; with their assumed scriptural support, they were incorporated into tradition; they finally received the sanction of high ecclesiastical courts and were henceforth regarded as final and infallible." [4] Thus the Bible came to be used not as a source of religious truth, but as a support for theological theories.

Dogmatic interpretation began to develop as early as the first decade of the second century and was crystallized in the Middle Ages. The method was used to support the unity and authority of the church. Dana and Glaze point out that Augustine urged that "in case a passage is difficult, one shall consider it first in the light of orthodoxy ('the rule of faith') and 'the authority of the church.' " [5] By this method all the doctrines of an authoritarian church were read into the Bible, and the true meaning of Scripture was soon lost in the traditional views of creedal orthodoxy.

Mystical Interpretation

Mystical interpretation is interpretation which seeks for "manifold depths and shades of meaning" [6] in Scripture and lays chief stress upon the devotional study of the Bible. Two leading representatives of this approach were the great medieval mystics, Hugo of St. Victor (d. 1141) and Bernard of Clairvaux (d. 1153). "The chief book of the mystics was the *Song of Songs* which they readily interpreted as the love affair of God and the

[3] H. E. Dana and R. E. Glaze, Jr., *Interpreting the New Testament* (Nashville: Broadman Press, 1961), p. 71.
[4] *Ibid.*
[5] *Ibid.*, p. 72.
[6] Milton S. Terry, *Biblical Hermeneutics* (Grand Rapids: Zondervan Publishing House, 1956), p. 164.

mystic resulting in the spiritual delights told in terms of physical delights." [7]

In the post-Reformation period the Pietists of Germany practiced mystical interpretation. They added a new element, claiming that interpretation was guided by an "inward light" received as "an unction from the Holy Spirit." It is possible to discard the rules of grammar and usage of words to discover what the internal light of the Spirit reveals in a certain passage. Quakers in England and America make use of this approach.

Mystical interpretation served a purpose in the Middle Ages as a reaction against strict dogmatic interpretation. It also emphasized the personal, spiritual, and devotional dimensions of Bible study. But it led to extreme allegorizing, to superficial interpretation, and to subjectivism.

Rationalistic Interpretation

Rationalistic interpretation embraced many different approaches to Scripture. "Rationalism . . . is that view which claims that the human intelligence is capable of discovering whatever truth there is to know, or of adequately testing whatever claims to be truth." [8] Rationalism was at its height in the middle of the nineteenth century and has greatly affected twentieth-century interpretation of Scripture.

Naturalistic interpretation.—Rationalism was best represented by the naturalistic interpretation of Scripture. Naturalism rejected all supernatural agency in human affairs, consequently rejecting miracles or apparent divine intervention in history. Paulus was a leader in this approach. In his commentary on the New Testament, "he rejects all supernatural agency in human affairs, and explains the miracles of Jesus either as acts of kindness, or exhibitions of medical skill, or illustrations of personal sagacity and tact, recorded in a manner peculiar to the age and opinions of the different writers." [9]

---

[7] Bernard Ramm, *Protestant Biblical Interpretation* (Boston: W. A. Wilde Co., 1950), pp. 33-34.

[8] *Ibid.,* p. 36

[9] Terry, *op. cit.,* p. 168.

Mythical interpretation.—Mythical interpretation, represented particularly by David Friedrich Strauss, is based on the assumption that the idea of God and truths of Christian faith were developed in the consciousness of humanity. Truths did not come as the result of revelation but as the result of development and discovery. Strauss's position is set forth in his *Life of Christ* in which he presents Christ as the mythical creation of the early church. "Adoring enthusiasts clothed the memory of the man Jesus with all that could enhance his name and character as the Messiah of the world." [10] The problem of the interpreter is to distinguish between fact and fiction.

The mythical approach to Scripture, however, breaks down of its own weight. The portrayal of Christ in Scripture is too perfect to be the product of human fancy. Men who penned Scripture could not have created such a remarkable person.

Accommodation theory of interpretation.—The accommodation theory of interpretation in general sets aside the supernatural. It attributes "miracles, vicarious and expiatory sacrifice, the resurrection, eternal judgment, and the existence of angels and demons . . . to . . . accommodation to the superstitious notions, prejudices, and ignorance of the times." [11] J. S. Semler was a representative of this type interpretation. He rejected the inspiration of the Scriptures and in general interpreted the teachings of the Old Testament, Matthew's Gospel, John's Gospel, and the writings of Paul as faulty and narrow and consequently of no enduring value.[12]

Moral interpretation.—Moral interpretation of the Scriptures is represented in the approach of Immanuel Kant. He studied the Bible chiefly for its moral and ethical content. Its theological significance was overlooked. This method of interpretation is obviously too subjective and inclines too much "to the peculiar faith or fancy of the interpreter." [13]

---

[10] *Ibid.*, p. 169.
[11] *Ibid.*, p. 166.
[12] *Ibid.*
[13] *Ibid.*, p. 167.

Modern Interpretation

Formgeschichte.—The modern approach to interpretation is represented by related yet distinct efforts to understand Scripture. In the background of contemporary interpretation is the approach of form criticism *(Formgeschichte)*. Form criticism is "an effort to distinguish the successive strata of primitive gospel tradition and detect the historical factors which influenced their production." [14] "Our Gospels are made up, according to *Formgeschichte*, of distinguishable blocks of tradition, which began first with detached illustrations, or 'paradigms,' used by the primitive Christian evangelists, then a stratum of stories, or Christian folklore, laid upon this, then a stratum of sayings grouped into lessons for didactic purpose, the whole embellished with legendary additions and interspersed with myths." [15] Thus, interpretation based on form criticism is an effort to recognize and explore the various strata of Scripture tradition.

Neo-orthodox interpretation.—Neo-orthodoxy in general rejects an infallible Bible and attempts to interpret Scripture mythologically. "By mythological is not meant the fanciful, or imaginative, but that the *myth* is a conveyer of theological truth in historical garb." [16] According to this view, the theological truth is not dependent on the historical garb in which it is presented. This results in a symbolic interpretation of Scripture.

Demythologizing and existential interpretation.—Rudolf Bultmann represents the process of interpretation called demythologizing. To demythologize *(entmythologistierung)* means "to take the myth out of, to free from mythology." According to Bultmann, the essence of the gospel, the *kerygma*, can be determined only by stripping away or identifying every element of myth which adheres to the gospel record. Myth in the Scriptures is that which is incompatible with the temper and outlook of this scientific era. Bultmann interprets Scripture from

---

[14] H. E. Dana, *Searching the Scriptures* (New Orleans: Bible Institute Memorial Press, 1936), p. 147.

[15] *Ibid.*

[16] Ramm, *op. cit.*, p. 43.

within the framework of existentialist philosophy. The true meaning of Scripture is its significance to man immediately involved in an experience of confrontation with God in Scripture.

Demythologizing is an effort to understand the meaning of Scripture in terms of its relevance to life. As a method of interpretation it has serious shortcomings. It appears to be an intellectual kind of allegorizing. It does tend to "fanciful allegorization." [17] In doing so it fails to give proper consideration to the historical integrity of Scripture. Denying the historicity of basic elements of the *kerygma* robs Christianity of its historical ground and character. It makes the "modern scientific mind" the criterion by which Scripture is discerned, rather than judging scientism by the Bible. Thus, it tends to become too subjective.

Grammatico-historical and Theological Interpretation

Sound interpretation of the Bible has been designated by different terms; it has been called "historical" and also "grammatico-historical." Historical interpretation found expression in early Christian centuries in the Syrian school which had its center in Antioch. Two significant representatives of this school were John Chrysostom (A.D. 347-407) and Theodore of Mopsuestia. It is said of Theodore that "he observed closely the literary details, such as grammatical constructions, rhetorical style, vocabulary, etc. He was a student of New Testament times, and paid considerable attention to evidences from contemporary life." [18] In later centuries the Reformers, Luther and Calvin, sought to interpret the Bible historically with due attention given to the grammar of the passage. By grammatico-historical interpretation is meant that interpretation of Scripture "required by the laws of grammar and the facts of history." [19] Some authors use the term "literal" to describe what they mean by grammatical.

---

[17] John Knox, *The Integrity of Preaching* (New York: Abingdon Press, 1957), 43.

[18] Dana, *op. cit.*, p. 70.

[19] Terry, *op. cit.*, p. 203.

Recent trends have emphasized theological interpretation—the effort to understand the essential truths of a passage of Scripture. Those who seek to interpret the Bible theologically range from those who see it simply as a necessary but imperfect vehicle to portray truth to those who take it seriously as well as the truths it presents. While the first group gives little attention to historical and literary exegesis, the second group is concerned about both in order to discover the theological truths of the passage. In this sense, theological interpretation is an essential part of grammatico-historical interpretation. True interpretation seeks to understand the truths of a passage of Scripture by careful grammatical analysis against its historical background.

The Steps in Interpretation

Interpretation is "the effort of one mind to follow the thought processes of another mind by means of symbols which we call language." [20] As applied to Scripture, interpretation is the effort to follow the thought processes of the Spirit-inspired writer through the language of Scripture.

The Text and Its Historical Background

To understand the language of Scripture it is necessary to place the passage in its historical setting. The author and his situation should be known and understood. The author of a passage had certain mental habits and distinctive views. He had his heritage of ideas. He wrote or spoke out of an immediate environment. All of these factors affected what he said and helped to determine the significance of what he wrote. To understand the man and his situation is to discover significance in the passage which could not otherwise be known.

A knowledge of the readers first addressed by the author is helpful to textual understanding. The heritage of ideas of the first readers, their character, mental habits, and the environment determined the manner in which the author addressed them and

---

[20] Dana and Glaze, *op. cit.*, p. 2.

influenced the ideas and terminology used to convey his thought.

To know the occasion and purpose of the writing will make the truths of the passage clearer. There was a situation which called forth the passage; the author had a reason for writing. To know these is to stand at a vantage point of understanding.

In addition to historical background, a passage may have historical content. There may be geographical, political, economic, and social conditions reflected in the passage. No true meaning can be assigned to it until the significance of these historical reflections is known. It is said of Mary and her relation to Joseph, "Mary, who was betrothed to him." Here is a reflection of first-century Jewish marriage customs. Before the situation can be correctly interpreted, the social customs of the Jews relating to marriage must be understood.

The Text and Its Context

To understand the language of Scripture, a passage must be placed in its context. "The *context* of a word or expression is that part of a discourse which is immediately connected with it, or that precedes or follows it." [21] The immediate context consists of those verses or paragraphs immediately preceding or following a passage. The remote context is that portion of Scripture less closely related to the passage and may embrace paragraphs, a chapter, or even an entire book of Scripture. Beyond the remote context there is the larger context of the development of thought in the Bible itself. The principle of progressive revelation calls for a passage being interpreted in the light of its relation to the stages of development of biblical peoples and writers.

It is easy to misinterpret Scripture by failure to relate a passage of its context. The context may be disregarded or it can be falsely interpreted. Consider the words of Paul in Colossians 2:21: "Touch not; taste not; handle not." These words have been used as the text for sermons on temperance, and they were

---

[21] Clinton Lockhart, *Principles of Interpretation* (Kansas City, Kan.: Central Seminary Press, 1901), p. 108.

at one time used as slogans for temperance societies. Actually these are not rules which Paul commends, but ascetic practices which he decries, saying, "Why . . . are ye subject to ordinances . . . after the commandments and doctrines of men?" (Col. 2:20-23). These are not injunctions to be obeyed but ascetic rules to be avoided.

The words of Jesus in John 12:32, "I, if I be lifted up from the earth, will draw all men unto me," have often been misapplied, if not misinterpreted. When Jesus spoke of "being lifted up," the explanation of this terminology is given in the next verse. "This he said, signifying what death he should die." The "being lifted up" is a reference to his death on the cross and not to his being lifted up in speech, living, or witnessing.

The Text and Its Analysis

Understanding the text itself is at the heart of interpretation. To understand the text the interpreter must know the kind of language with which he deals, the significance of words, and the relation of the words to each other in the passage. One of the first problems of the interpreter is to determine the kind of language with which he is working. Is it prose or poetry? Is it literal or figurative? Is it literal but containing figures of speech? Different kinds of language are differently interpreted. Mistakes have often been made by interpreting literal passages as figurative or figurative passages as literal. It is also possible to press a figure of speech too far. To interpret poetry as prose is to open the door for all kinds of misunderstanding.

The first step toward understanding a passage is knowing the meaning of its words. Dictionaries and lexicons are basic guides at this point. Having observed the meaning of a word, the interpreter is then wise to check the word in a concordance to observe its use in other passages. Word study books and commentaries assist in the understanding of the language of the passage. Errors are frequently made by the interpreter because of his failure to understand the meaning of words. In the King James translation Philippians 1:27 reads, "Only let your conver-

sation be as it becometh the gospel of Christ." Some preachers
have used this as a text for the subject, "How Christians Ought
to Talk." The American Standard translation reveals the error
of this interpretation, "Only let your manner of life be worthy
of the gospel of Christ." The marginal reading is: "Only behave
as citizens worthily of the gospel of Christ." Another text commonly misinterpreted is 2 Timothy 2:15, "Study to shew thyself
approved unto God." The word "study" is often misunderstood.
Again, the American Standard translation helps. "Give diligence
to present thyself approved unto God." To "study" in this
passage means to give "studied" or diligent effort.

Grammatical relations within the passage must be clear if the
passage is to be understood. Words mean what they mean as
they stand in relation to each other. The words must be studied
in their relationships. A simple exercise is to diagram the text and
parse the forms appearing in it. This will demonstrate the relationship of all words in the text to each other. Other significant
grammatical points to observe are the devices for emphasis and
the function of the different tenses. A simple error is frequently
made in interpreting Ephesians 2:8, "For by grace are ye saved
through faith; and that not of yourselves." To what does "that"
refer? The common answer is to say "faith," but the word can
refer to neither faith nor grace in the previous part of the verse.
These words are feminine in Greek while the word for "that"
is neuter. "That" must refer to the idea of salvation expressed in
the first part of the verse. "And *that* [the salvation referred to]
is not of yourselves; it is the gift of God."

To understand a passage, it is also helpful, if not necessary, to
understand the mood and spirit of the passage. The atmosphere
of the passage should be recreated.[22] "Some passages reflect a
mood of judgment, some of courage, some of quiet confidence,
others of righteous indignation at some wrong." [23] To interpret
correctly one must perceive and understand this mood. Donald
Miller says that there are ways in which the mood of a passage

[22] Miller, *The Way to Biblical Preaching*, pp. 142-53.
[23] *Ibid.*, p. 147.

is captured. "First, it may be well to cultivate the imagination until one is enabled to enter into the biblical scenes and feel the throb of the heartbeat of the biblical characters. . . . The second suggestion is that this should be rooted in prolonged and intimate touch with the passage of Scripture on which one is planning to preach." [24] To understand the mood of a passage the interpreter should make careful investigation of its historical background, know the nature of the language it contains, and carefully place it in its context. The pervading spirit of a passage helps to shape its meaning and determine its significance.

To interpret correctly, attention should be given to comparative passages. There may be other references that seem to contradict what appears to be the meaning of the passage. The conservative interpreter will seek to harmonize the two. An illustration is found in the teachings of Paul and James on the doctrine of justification by faith. Some passages will agree with and enlarge the idea contained in the text, and they must be checked for their value in enlarging the area of truth involved in the message. For comparative passages the interpreter should turn to the concordance and to his commentaries. Most standard commentaries will refer to contrasting or comparative passages.

The Text and Its Truths

After taking these steps toward understanding, the interpreter is prepared to draw truths and applications from the passage. He should state the central truth of his text for himself and list the truths involved in it. This is doctrinal interpretation. He should attempt to put in one clear, concise sentence what he believes to be the central idea of the passage. This is not easy, but it is an exercise which is exceedingly fruitful from a sermonic point of view. With the central truth in mind, the interpreter should list what he considers to be the several significant truths of the passage.

After doctrinal investigation the next step is practical interpretation. The possible applications of the passage to the needs

[24] *Ibid.,* p. 146.

of the people should be listed. The preacher should ask himself
the question, "At what points does this passage touch the lives
of my people?" He should then list these points for possible use
later. The following form for the above exercise is recommended:

Scripture passage: John 4:1-43
Central truth: God is Spirit. All men may come to him anywhere or
any time through Christ.

Truths of the Passage	Applications of Life Experiences
God is Spirit	Lack of understanding about God
Worship is a matter of spirit	Inadequate conceptions of worship
God is universal (the God of all men)	National and racial prejudices
Salvation (transformation of life) is of Christ	Lack of spiritual understanding
All men are significant in God's eyes	Needy fields for witnessing

Using a sheet of paper lined down the center, the preacher
places on one side of the sheet the truths he has discovered in
the passage and on the other side the relationship of these truths
to life. He will soon discover that such an exercise is exceedingly
fruitful for preaching.

Different men have various ways of approaching a passage for
study. The following program is offered as a suggested pattern
to be used or modified as a man sees fit.

The interpreter begins with a careful reading of the passages
in English, possibly in as many English translations as are available. If possible, he should then translate the passage from the
Greek or Hebrew.

Then he interprets the passage carefully for himself. He wants
his first serious thinking about the passage to be his own. When
he feels that he has thought through the passage for himself, he
then investigates the passage in the available commentaries. He

should begin with critical and exegetical commentaries and then
turn to the expository commentaries, and from these to the devotional ones. He should carefully take notes on the material
which he discovers.

After commentary investigation, the interpreter will then
turn to the rest of his library to study through any other material which discusses the passage. There are such sources as
periodical material and books of sermons. He should carefully
glean through these for whatever help they may offer.

During this process the preacher should adopt some means
acceptable and usable to himself for taking notes. He may use
3 by 5 or 4 by 6 cards. He may pefer to use 8½ by 11 sheets of
paper. Usually only one idea or discussion of one verse of Scripture should be placed on each card. The preacher should be
especially careful to record and preserve his own independent
thinking about the passage. He should record any outline possibilities or sermonic applications of the passage. He later may find
such material of value.

The Principles of Interpretation

When the preacher interprets Scripture he must recognize its
twofold character.[25] Scripture should be recognized as revelation
from God, and, thus, of divine character. It should also be
recognized as a revelation mediated through human agency,
thus having human character. The principles of interpretation
are determined by this twofold aspect of Scripture.

The Bible is a revelation from God, inspired by the Holy
Spirit, and communicated to man for the purpose of redemption.
Thus, "the interpreter should reverently contemplate the mind
of the Spirit as conveyed in the thought of the writer." [26] Scripture is viewed as God's message to man, and the interpreter seeks
to discover what God is saying.

The interpreter of the Bible should interpret it as a unified
whole, centered in God's redemptive message. Believing in the

---

[25] Dana and Glaze, *op. cit.*, p. 126.
[26] *Ibid.*, p. 128.

unity of the Bible, the reverent interpreter seeks to interpret it in consistency with itself.

As divine revelation the Bible contains passages of predictive import. They are expressed in the thought forms and against the historical background of the writers. They are best understood in the light of those thought forms and historical background. Great care should be exercised to distinguish between predictive and nonpredictive passages.

Because Scripture is divine revelation, miracles are accepted as possible and interpreted in light of the author's purpose in recording them. Miracles in the Bible generally attest the validity of the message as divine. They have a kind of apologetic value but are actually to be viewed as more than this. They are an inherent part of the divine revelation.

The divine nature of Scripture is a fundamental assumption; this conviction serves as a kind of North Star for reverent interpretation of the Bible. At the same time the preacher must also realize that this revelation is mediated through human agency.

Although the redemptive message of the Scriptures originated in the mind of the Spirit, it has been delivered to man through normal human processes, and is, therefore, characteristically human. As such, it is to be interpreted by the use of the same general principles which would be employed for the understanding of any other literature.[27]

The interpreter should seek to understand what the author meant. Under the inspiration of the Holy Spirit the writers of Scripture wrote as intelligent men. They were attempting to express the truth of God as they understood it under divine inspiration. Their messages were intelligent and intelligible. They meant something to an audience of people who first received them. The true import of a passage is what the author of the passage intended that it should mean to those to whom he wrote. Simple honesty must lead the interpreter to ask: What did Paul,

---

[27] *Ibid.*, p. 133.

John, or James mean when he penned these words? What they
meant to him is the true significance of the passage.

There is a second question to ask: "What does this passage
mean to me?" The simple, obvious meaning of a passage should
usually be accepted as its true meaning unless there are strong
reasons for looking for a different significance. The biblical
writers were not attempting to obscure thought or to speak in
riddles. Rather they were attempting to communicate a message.
Assuming that they were intelligent men, led by the intelligent
Spirit, it follows that their messages are intelligible.

A passage should be interpreted as presenting only one meaning. As intelligent men, writers of Scripture attempted to convey
intelligible meaning. Scripture does not contain double meanings, except perhaps in apocalyptic literature. The historical
context for that type led its 'writers to couch their thought in
mysterious language. Their images may appear literally to mean
one thing while in reality the passage has a highly figurative
significance. This is not, however, the usual language of the
Bible. A Scripture passage normally has one meaning, and this
meaning is usually the literal one.

An author should be interpreted in consistency with himself.
It is not likely that an author would contradict his own writing.
This is an assumption of everyday human experience. Add to
this the factor of divine inspiration, and the two together assure
consistency and harmony in the thought of Scripture. An
author's general line of thought and his expressed ideas will help
to determine what he means in a particular passage which appears to contradict previously expressed thought.

Historical background and content should be given due consideration in interpreting a passage. Scripture writers spoke out
of a definite historical context. They themselves were historically
rooted. They often spoke to historical occasions and situations.
They often had definite historical purposes in writing. The historical circumstances definitely influenced the meaning of the
writer and his words. To understand any passage, the preacher
must study this historical environment.

The contextual relations of a passage also should be given due attention. Normally, the ideas of Scripture are presented in continuity of narrative or thesis. Exceptions to this principle would be the book of Proverbs and other wisdom books. The varied ideas in such books must be understood in the light of the units of thought of which they are a part. The simplest way to misinterpret is to isolate a passage from its context. It is supremely important for the interpreter to understand the developing thought of a Bible book. He should outline the book for himself before he embarks on the task of interpretation.

The language of Scripture should be understood in the light of the meaning of the language in the author's times. Biblical writers wrote for the people of their day, and they must have used words which were intelligible to those people. To assign an earlier meaning to a word or to adopt a developed meaning would be to misinterpret the passage. Careful consideration should be given to the use of the word in the day of the author. Increasing possibilities in this respect are opening up with new archeological discoveries and new investigation of papyri.

The literary style of the language of Scripture is a factor in sound interpretation. To interpret correctly, prose must be interpreted as prose, poetry as poetry, literal language as literal, and figurative language as figurative. The interpreter should recognize the literary quality of the language which he is seeking to interpret.

The Text and the Idea of the Sermon

When the preacher has interpreted his passage, he is ready to begin to phrase the final form of the idea of the sermon. If it is to be a biblical message, the idea of the sermon must be found in and based on the passage of Scripture.

The idea of the sermon may be directly contained in the text.[28] A thought expressed in the passage may become the idea of the sermon. The thought may be the central thought of the

---

[28] See Jeff D. Ray, *Expository Preaching* (Grand Rapids: Zondervan Publishing House, 1939), pp. 101-10.

passage or it may be a related or subordinate thought. In John 3:7 Jesus said, "Ye must be born again." The central truth here is *the necessity of the new birth.* This idea is directly contained in the passage, and in the truest kind of biblical preaching this would be the theme of a sermon based on this passage.

To discover a sermonic idea directly contained in the passage, the minister should attempt to express the central truth of the passage in one clear, concise, declarative sentence. Take the third chapter of John as an example. Its central truth could be expressed in this fashion: *Regardless of character or culture every man needs a transforming experience of regeneration wrought in his life by the Holy Spirit of God.*

Other preaching ideas may be discovered by asking what other truths in the passage have significance for life experience. It is possible to find sermonic ideas in the subordinate truths implicitly contained in the passage. Such ideas are genuinely biblical.

Sermonic ideas may also be drawn from passages by logical inference through deduction or induction.

Deduction means the process of reasoning by which the interpreter proceeds from the general thought to the particular to develop his sermon theme. A general idea in the passage becomes the basis of a particular idea for preaching. The text may state a general truth which is applied to a particular idea in the sermon. Romans 12:9 contains the general injunction, "Abhor that which is evil." One may use this passage as a text to suggest what a Christian's attitude toward any evil should be, provided, of course, that he could prove that it was evil. Romans 14:23 reads: "Whatsoever is not of faith is sin." Christians could be challenged to forsake as sin those things that could not be demonstrated to be of faith.

Induction means that process of reasoning in which the interpreter proceeds from the particular idea in Scripture to a general principle drawn from it. A specific experience in the passage becomes the grounds for a general truth drawn from it. This is a common way of using Scripture.

On the basis of the experience of the rich fool in Luke 12:19-20 one could preach on "The Futility of Covetousness." Paul's discussion of the eating of meat offered to idols could be used to discuss "The Obligations of Christian Influence." The experience of Daniel in refusing to eat of the king's meat and finding in the refusal the blessing of God could become the basis of a sermon on the principle of "Blessing Through Loyalty."

Sermon ideas may be derived through analogical deduction. The argument from analogy is based on the assumption that two things are so alike in nature and function that what we know to be true of one we infer to be true of the other. In Matthew 18:15-17 there is a discussion of the means of settling personal difficulties. By way of analogy this same approach could be applied to the relationship of nations under the subject "The Ways of Preventing War."

Sermon ideas may also be derived from passages by way of suggestion. The idea cannot be said to be contained or inferred from the text. At best it can only be said that the text suggests the idea. This method is fraught with dangers and is to be carefully used. If the suggestion is natural and not overdrawn, then the method is legitimate. Bushnell's sermon, "Unconscious Influence," is based on John 20:8, "Then went in also that other disciple." The best that can be said for the subject is that it is suggested by the passage. Yet that suggestion proved to be the beginning of a significant sermon. Fosdick's sermon, "Christians in Spite of Everything," is based on Philippians 4:22, "All the saints salute you, chiefly they that are of Caesar's household." In following the lead of a suggestion, the preacher must be sure that the mental path between the text and the subject is clear.

The sermon began as an idea in the mind and heart of the preacher. It was related to a passage of Scripture, thoroughly studied and understood. Then the initial idea was formulated into a thesis or affirmation and was related to an objective in the experience of the people. With the central truth of the passage formulated in a thesis and related to an objective, the preacher is now ready to gather material for developing the sermon.

IV

Gathering Material

The primary source of material for the sermon is the Bible. Careful exegesis of the passage on which the sermon is to be based will provide abundant material for use. But some ideas, thoughts, and illustrations in the sermon will come from other sources. Literature, history, science, and personal experience will suggest ideas and illustrations to help make the sermon intelligible and appealing to the hearer.

Studying for Sermon Preparation

A General Program of Study

Material for preaching will grow out of the preacher's consistent and diligent program of study. Throughout his ministry the preacher will engage in a general program of study, not necessarily related to the immediate preparation of specific sermons. It will include reading of broad scope, from classical literature to the daily paper. In the great classics of world literature there is abundance of grist for the preacher's mill. Reading current magazines and periodicals helps to keep the preacher acquainted with the times in which he lives. It can be done at times specifically set aside. Both kinds of reading can be done on a regular planned schedule, or they can be picked up in the spare moments that are often wasted. Diligent and conscientious planning will afford valuable time for general reading.

A Program of Bible Study

The general program of study should include a continuing exegetical and expository study of the Bible. The preacher should work out a program of study covering a period of years which would enable him to give attention to all areas of biblical material. Persistent study of the text of the Bible should occasionally give way to topical study. The preacher should explore the great themes of the Word of God. He may use the processes of systematic theology or biblical theology in developing topical research. Abundant material for preaching will arise from such a program of exegetical and topical study of the Bible.

A Program of Sermon Preparation

Of course the preacher must follow a specific program of study for the preparation of each sermon. The nature of such a program will vary with each man because of differences in temperament, disposition, and habits of work.

Ralph W. Sockman describes his method by saying that he sows the ideas for his sermons in the summer and returns to his work in the fall with seventy-five or a hundred sermon themes in mind. He then frequently goes over these to see "which ones seem to be sprouting." [1] He devotes three days of the week to the sermon he is to preach on Sunday morning, putting in approximately eighteen hours of study on each sermon. He consults books in his library dealing with the sermon. When this material has been gathered, he then proceeds to organize the sermon outline. This he does on Friday night, leaving the writing of the sermon to Saturday.

R. G. Lee begins, as he expresses it, by reading the Bible "with prayer in my heart that God will direct me to the choice of a subject and a text upon which to pitch my mental tent." When the subject and text are chosen, he then develops an outline, doing the "best thinking I can on the passage." In doing so he searches the Bible for "substantiating statements of God's truth." [2]

When this is done, he reads what other men have said about

---

[1] "A Statement of My Method," in Macleod, *op. cit.*, p. 181.
[2] H. C. Brown, Jr. (ed.), *Southern Baptist Preaching* (Nashville: Broadman Press, 1959), pp. 112-13.

the subject, but he says, "I'm not a slave to commentaries." [3]
This study is followed by the gathering of related truths from
any realm—history, biography, poetry, philosophy. He even
seeks statements which are contrary to his own convictions. He
tries to prepare his sermons with the needs of people in mind:
lost people, brokenhearted people, people in despair, complacent people. He attempts also to prepare all sermons with Jesus
as the central theme and often asks himself the question: What
does Jesus think of this? With this background of preparation
in hand he then writes his sermon in full.

It is interesting to observe how often those who discuss their
ways of selecting sermon topics and ideas refer to some method
of giving ideas an opportunity to grow and develop. H. Guy
Moore [4] speaks of a "seed plot" for future sermons. This is a
drawer where he places ideas, sermons, parts of series, and illustrations as they come to him. C. Roy Angell [5] speaks of a clip
board in his study on which he writes at the top of a blank page:
a text, an incident, a sermon topic that has occurred to him.
Sometimes he may have as many as fifty pages on this clip board.
He goes over these each week prayerfully waiting for guidance
in selecting one for a future sermon. Duke McCall says that
when an insight, idea, or message grips him and fires his imagination, he immediately writes it down. Sometimes he dictates a
page or two to enlarge the idea. Such material is placed in a
folder "where it may stay for a few days or a few years until a
preaching opportunity seems to be the suitable occasion for the
sermon." [6]

Gathering Illustrations for the Sermon

A significant and pleasant task in developing material for sermons is the gathering of illustrations. To illustrate means to
throw light (luster) upon a subject or an idea; an illustration

---

[3] *Ibid.*, p. 113.
[4] *Ibid.*, p. 139.
[5] *Ibid.*, p. 21.
[6] *Ibid.*, p. 122.

is any device to accomplish this purpose. Illustrations are to sermons what windows are to houses; they let light in upon the otherwise obscure ideas of the message.

The Need for Illustrations

Illustrations are needed in sermons. They are needed to reach the present-day "picture-conscious" mind. Our generation has been trained to think in pictures. Children are taught to read by the use of visual aids. The earliest lessons in school are learned through the devices of visual projection. Motion pictures and television have further trained the modern mind to think in pictures. Minds so trained will not listen through a sermon wholly dependent upon logical thought to convey its meaning. People need word pictures in preaching, too.

Illustrations are needed in sermons to clarify the essential truths of the Christian faith. A thoughtful review of the central conceptions of Christian truth will reveal that they are often presented in images. The cross, baptism, the Lord's Supper are symbols. They convey the truth in the form of images. No man can speak adequately of the Christian faith without the use of illustrations, for its basic elements are expressed in the form of pictures.

Illustrations are needed in sermons to make a more permanent impression for the truth. It has been discovered that people remember illustrations in a sermon longer than they do any other of its elements. Clarence E. Macartney tells of the experience of a minister who asked twenty people to write down what they could remember of a sermon which he had preached some months before. Only one or two remembered the outline or other features of the sermon. Nearly everyone remembered the closing illustration.[7]

To use illustrations in sermons is to follow the example of Jesus, the Master Teacher. His messages were filled with all types and kinds of illustrations. There are metaphors, similes,

---

[7] *Preaching Without Notes* (Nashville: Abingdon-Cokesbury Press, 1946), p. 33.

and other figures of speech. There are stories and illustrative references taken from the common life of the people. He spoke of women baking bread or sweeping the house. He spoke of the sower in the field, the common weather proverbs, the merchant of pearls. He described children at play in the market places and called attention to the flowers of the field and the birds of the heavens. The common people's response to Jesus can be partly explained by the simple illustrative way in which he taught.

Illustrations are used in sermons to explain. Truths are made clear and are understood by the use of illustrations. By starting with a familiar experience the preacher can lead his people to understand what is not known. To cite examples is one of the most effective ways to make clear an abstract truth presented in the message.

Illustrations are used to prove a point. Occasionally in preaching it is necessary for the preacher to reason with his audience in order to establish a truth. Often the simplest and most effective argument is illustration. Examples of the truth may be presented. Demonstrations of the truth may be set forth. Analogies that will help to support the truth can be presented. Often the hearers are willing to accept an idea when they can say in response to it, "I see."

Illustrations are used to attract or to arouse attention. At the beginning of a message an illustration can be used to gain attention. At intervals in the message illustrations serve to arouse wavering attention. People listen to illustrations even when they do not listen to the rest of the message.

Illustrations are used to kindle emotional response. Some illustrations have the capacity to touch the hearts of individuals. There is a legitimate and constructive kindling of the emotions. Illustrations in a peculiar way possess the power to arouse emotional response.

Types of Illustrations

Illustrations may take various forms. Thought of as any device of language designed to throw light on the truth, illustrations are words or word combinations designed to create mental images of the truth, frequently with some appeal to the senses or emotions.

Consequently an illustration may consist of one striking and picturesque word. One word, concrete in nature and well placed in the sentence, will create a picture of that which the preacher wishes to express. R. G. Lee speaks of a "Cross swaying in the darkness with a white, blood-splotched, naked body upon it." [8] Here mere adjectives, "white," "blood-splotched," and "naked," paint an entire portrait.

Illustrations may consist of striking and unusual combinations of words. Dawson C. Bryan [9] cites from a *Reader's Digest* column entitled "Towards a More Picturesque Speech" some examples of unusual word combinations: "Red-haired autumn." "The day snailed by." "The wrinkled half of my life." "The bells and clocks of the town were discussing midnight." "Abrupt as a slammed door." "Irrevocable as a haircut." "As involved as spaghetti."

These striking and picturesque words and combinations of words may be either metaphor or simile. A metaphor is a figure of speech by which a word or phrase literally denoting one thing is applied to another to suggest a likeness between them. Metaphors are often used in the Scriptures. They appear particularly in the teaching of Jesus. Bryan says that there are fifty-six metaphors in the Sermon on the Mount.[10] "Ye are the salt of the earth." "Ye are the light of the world." These are two of the most graphic and well-known metaphors of Jesus. Such metaphors as "I am the good shepherd," "I am the door," "I am the water of life" indicate Jesus' fondness for the use of this form of graphic speech.

A simile is a figure of speech in which the likeness of things is expressed. Jesus often made use of similes. His parabolic de-

---

[8] Brown, *Southern Baptist Preaching*, p. 119.

[9] *The Art of Illustrating Sermons* (Nashville: Abingdon-Cokesbury Press, 1938), p. 56.

[10] *Ibid.*, p. 55.

scriptions of the kingdom of heaven often are similes. He compared his generation to children playing in the market place. Again, Bryan calls attention to similes selected from some modern sermons: "As futile as an old mistake." "As vague and meaningless as an embalmed deity." [11]

An illustration may take the form of a story or narrative. It may be a historical event presented in the form of a story, or it may be an incident, a fable, a parable, or a personal experience. The story or anecdote has been a favorite mode of conveying thought as long as men have sought to communicate with each other. Stories have almost universal appeal, but there is an art to telling them. They are not easy to tell effectively. But when a story is well done, there is no more effective and forceful means of communication. The story seems to have been George W. Truett's favorite mode of illustration. A survey of his sermons for an understanding of his use of the story in preaching is a rewarding study.

Poems also may be used as illustrations. In poetry, truth can be expressed in beautiful and imaginistic language, concisely and effectively phrased. Using poetry to illustrate will not only help to illuminate but will add beauty to the truth expressed. There is an almost universally favorable response to poetry. Consequently, the use of the poem as an illustration is an effective and attractive way to make the truth clear.

Sources of Illustrations

Illustrations for sermons may come from anywhere. Broadus said, "Illustration of religious truth may be drawn from the whole realm of existence and of conception." [12] Someone asked, "Where do illustrations come from?" The answer is "from anywhere and everywhere."

The Bible is a primary source of illustration. Dawson Byran says, "Within the library of Scripture is every conceivable type of illustration on every subject or theme which the preacher

[11] *Ibid.*
[12] *On the Preparation and Delivery of Sermons,* p. 199.

shall touch." [13] Turning to the Bible for illustrations has many advantages. Biblical illustrations are abundant. In the Bible men of all kinds and types have met God and experienced life in almost every conceivable circumstance. Biblical illustrations are familiar without being trite. A certain amount of familiarity with an illustration makes it more effective. Biblical illustrations are characterized by a quality of authority. The fact that an illustration is drawn from the Bible gives it authority with many people which an illustration from another source would not have. Biblical illustrations have a remarkably timeless and contemporary quality about them. While biblical scenes may be garbed in the atmosphere and customs of thousands of years ago, the essential experiences of the men and women of Scripture speak to every era. The twentieth-century Christian often sees himself and his experience in a biblical character. The minister has in his Bible a treasure house of illustrative material.

Illustrations may be found also in literature. Biography and autobiography will yield abundant and useful illustrations. In their life stories men and women of God have laid open their souls as they interpret their own experiences with God and men. In autobiography we learn not only the facts of an individual's life but also the inner feelings and emotions of the individual in the midst of life's experiences. Such autobiographical classics as *The Journal of John Wesley*, *The Confessions of St. Augustine*, *The Autobiography of Mark Rutherford*, and Albert Schweitzer's *Out of My Life and Thought* abound in illustrative material.

In biography the lives of men are interpreted by others. Sometimes biographies are too eulogistic or too realistic to be objectively true. Allowing for this, the minister may find great help in the lives of the great men and women of God. When asked what type reading he engaged in most, Fosdick replied, "Biography." Some interesting biographical sketches are found in W. L. Stidger's *The Human Side of Greatness* and A. D.

---

[13] Bryan, *op. cit.*, p. 93.

White's *Seven Great Statesmen in the Warfare of Humanity with Unreason.* These and many other sources will furnish the preacher with abundant illustrative material.

Fiction, too, is a rich resource for illustrations. Novelists attempt to portray life as people live it. They picture the hopes and aspirations of people, their defeats and tragedies, their joys and triumphs. Under a skilled pen even common experiences are graphically unfolded. As vivid portrayals of human experience, novels offer abundant material for illustrating spiritual realities. This is true primarily of classic fiction although there is some value in modern fiction. Note such novels as those of Nathaniel Hawthorne, *The Minister's Black Veil* and *The Marble Faun;* George Eliot, *The Mill on the Floss;* Charles Dickens, *David Copperfield.*

Drama is a bountiful source of sermon illustrations. It comes to grips with life in a realistic fashion to reveal the emotions, thoughts, and motives of the characters involved. Excerpts of the dialogue can be most effective when read well.

Essays of such men as Bacon, Emerson, and Macaulay provide abundant resources for quotations.

Poetry is one of the most useful sources of sermon illustrations. The minister may range the whole field of poetry—both classic and modern. He should use the great masterpieces of poetry but beware of the shallow though popular doggerel. The great poets of the centuries have framed great truths in a rich variety of poetic forms. The minister should read individually from some of the great poets of every century. He may also take advantage of the collections that have been made of the world's great religious poems. *Quotable Poems* (2 vols.) edited by Clark and Gillespie is now available in one volume entitled 1000 *Quotable Poems.* Caroline Hill has a volume, *The World's Great Religious Poetry.* The book, *Christ and the Fine Arts,* by Maus will provide helpful material.

Helpful illustrative material may be found in fables, myths, and legends. In the past greater use was made of myth and fable. In view of the current neglect of these areas, there may be a relatively new source of illustrations for contemporary use in preaching.

Illustrations may be drawn from the personal experiences of the preacher. His observations of nature and life about him offer abundant illustrations of the truths of God. The open-minded observer will discover these illustrations easily. His pastoral contacts offer innumerable opportunities for the discovery of sermon illustrations. Even his own spiritual experiences will yield sermonic illustrations. How did he find God in conversion? What was the nature of his call to preach? In what ways and what kind of experiences has God been made real to him? These may be very helpful when told to others. The pastor's travel experience, if not used excessively, can yield illustrative material.

Illustrations taken from personal experience have both advantages and disadvantages. Personal illustrations growing out of the preacher's own experience with God give to his preaching the quality of witness. All effective preaching must have this quality whether it contains personal illustrations or not. Personal illustrations are real and significant to the preacher. When wisely used, they give to preaching the quality of earnestness and involvement. If those who hear love and respect the preacher, his personal illustrations will have a significant force.

But personal illustrations may call attention to the preacher himself rather than to the truth he wishes to illustrate. Usually, it is the manner of telling the story that leaves the egotistical impression. Personal illustrations can easily be used too often. The preacher, his family, and his experiences may be paraded through the sermon. Personal illustrations have been known to "grow." The preacher may become guilty of exaggeration. An old-timer who had heard many preachers speak complimented an older preacher by saying, "I heard him use the same illustrations many times, but he always told them exactly the same way. They didn't grow." Then with a mischievous twinkle in his eyes he added, "Some preachers' stories do, you know." Preachers have been known to appropriate someone else's ex-

perience and report it as if it were their own. To do so is to seek
to portray truth by an untruth.

Illustrations may be drawn from history, both church history and secular history. Newspapers and news magazines are
valuable resources for illustrations drawn from contemporary
history. People are interested in history, past or present, particularly when history concerns persons. There is a kind of
fascination associated with personalities from the past. Such
persons are at least vaguely familiar to the preacher's audience,
and their stories will help focus attention on the truth to be
illustrated.

Illustrations may be seen in science. Men have always been
curious about natural phenomena, but in our time a heightened
emphasis on science has given new appeal to all scientific facts.
Add to this the reputation of science as being authoritative in
most areas of truth, and the force of a scientific illustration
becomes even more apparent.

One pitfall needs to be avoided. In the use of scientific material, the preacher should be certain that he is accurate. This
may be a problem if he did his own scientific studies a few
years ago. His scientific knowledge might be limited and out of
date. He could appear very foolish and lose effectiveness if he
were caught in error about science.

Illustrations may be found in the arts. Music offers abundant
opportunities. In the stories of hymns and hymn tunes are
valuable and moving illustrations. Stories of the great oratorios
have thrilled many people. Quoting hymns can illuminate many
dark sermonic passages. Stories about the painting of great masterpieces can also illustrate spiritual truths. Facts in the lives of
great artists may yield invaluable lessons. Effective illustrative
help may be found in descriptions of what one can see in the
great masterpieces. If one is not able to view the originals, he
can secure a volume which reproduces the originals. A careful
study of such a volume will sharpen a preacher's imagination
and appreciation.

Illustrations may be taken from books of sermons and books

of illustrations. Usually books of illustrations are not helpful. (The illustrations often lack life setting and are cold and lifeless.) While such books occasionally may give some effective help, books of sermons are better sources. In sermons the illustrations are found within real preaching contexts and in real life situations. They have a vitality not found in books of illustrations.

Illustrations may be created. If the preacher cannot find an illustration which aptly expresses what he wishes, he may create one out of his own imagination. This is acceptable if the preacher does not pretend that the illustration actually occurred and if the truth which it illustrates is not dependent on the fact that it did occur. It would be best to introduce such an illustration by a remark which would identify it as imaginary. The preacher could begin by saying, "Suppose," or "Imagine." Such created illustrations must be credible, that is, they must be so told that the audience can believe that they could have or might have taken place.

The Qualities of Good Illustrations

Webb B. Garrison in his book, *The Preacher and His Audience*,[14] sets out what he calls the criteria of the "good" illustration. An illustration, he says, should be understandable. It must start from an "island of experience" in the mind of the listener. It proceeds from the known to the unknown in the hearer's experience. Because of this point of contact in the hearer's life, the illustration is intelligible to him.

A good illustration is pertinent. It is applicable to the point being illustrated. A good question to ask of any illustration is whether or not it actually illustrates the point under discussion. A good illustration is fresh. It should possess an intrinsic freshness or at least create a new twist to an old idea. This will give vitality or aliveness to it. A good illustration should be convincing or credible. It must be possible for the audience to believe

---

[14] Westwood, N.J.: Fleming H. Revell Co., 1954, pp. 178-83.

that the experience actually occurred or could have occurred. A good illustration must be commensurate with the theme. Experiences may illustrate the point well but be of such nature as to violate the essential dignity of the theme. "Any illustration that cheapens the argument, or tends to divert the listener's mind into less exalted channels, should be avoided." [15] An illustration which has these qualities will have interest value. It will compel attention. In doing so it will effectively explain, prove, or enforce the truth the preacher desires to present.

Suggestions About the Use of Illustrations

The preacher should be careful not to use too many illustrations. Thought is diluted in force when the number of illustrations is multiplied. Someone has suggested that no more than one major illustration for each point is ideal, allowing another one for either the introduction or the conclusion. Bishop Boaz of the Methodist Church summarized his theory of effective preaching thus: the preacher should do three things with each point in the sermon: (1) make the point; (2) illustrate it; (3) apply it.

As a general rule, it is wise for the preacher not to talk about illustrating but just illustrate. Often long and sometimes apologetic introductions to illustrations destroy their effectiveness. To say, "Let me illustrate," or "Let me tell you this story to show what I mean," is to lose the attention of the audience.

Illustrations should be carefully planned, carefully selected, and carefully prepared for the most effective use. Too often illustrations are afterthoughts in sermons arising from the extemporaneous impulse of the preacher. It takes time to discover the right illustration. It takes care to build it into the sermon.[16]

Illustrations should be varied in types and sources. They should be selected from all areas of life and from many of the above sources. The preacher should check himself occasionally

---

[15] *Ibid.*, pp. 189-90.
[16] See Bryan, *op. cit.*, pp. 163-97.

in this respect. He may discover that he is repeating himself or that he is selecting his illustrations from a limited area of experience.

The preacher should cultivate the art of telling stories. It has been too often assumed that it is easy to tell a story effectively. This is far from true. There is real art in effective storytelling. The preacher should study a book on the art of telling stories. He can help himself greatly by practice in telling stories to children.

Almost all great preaching is characterized by the effective use of illustrations. The man who wishes to preach well will cultivate the art of illustrating his sermons.

Preserving the Sermon Material

Such a program of study and research will result in the discovery and accumulation of considerable material. What a waste of valuable time and energy if this material were simply discarded. Serious exegetical work has been done, illustrations gathered, and ideas developed and expanded—all these are worthy of preservation.

Some time in the future such material can be used again. The exegetical work done for one particular sermon may be used in the development of an entirely different one directed toward another situation. Good ideas developed now may serve good purposes at a later date. The same illustrations can be used on different occasions, but the preacher must recall that illustrations are remembered long after logic has dissolved. It is possible that a particular sermon will be used again. A sermon worth preaching once is worth preaching again. If a man has preserved his study material for a particular sermon, his preparation for the second preaching of that sermon can be more significant and valuable.

The manner of preserving material is a peculiarly individual matter. There are people of gifted memory. They need little more than to have heard or read something for it to be at their memory tip for use. This explains the fact that not infrequently you read an author who disparages the idea of filing material for preservation. Other people are gifted with a knack for details. They enjoy the work of filing, indexing, and cross-indexing. Still others need to preserve material but lack the disposition and discipline to follow an elaborate program of filing and indexing.

Because of differing abilities and personalities, one's method of preserving material must be distinctly his own. This does not mean that he will develop his own original system, but that he will adopt a system that fits his own personality, one which he can and will use.

The man with photographic memory needs to do little except read and remember. Some have assisted themselves in this respect by making it a practice to index books (as they read them) on the inside cover of the book or on the flyleaf. Such a student usually remembers the book in which current material is to be found. He then turns to the subject index on the flyleaf of the book and locates the page on which the material is to be found.

The man with the gift for attention to details can use elaborate and detailed methods of filing and indexing. He needs time to set aside to keep his filing and indexing up to date. He needs occasionally to review the material filed and indexed with a view to discarding some of it. It is possible to keep filed material alive and vital. In a special way one's library is placed at his fingertips through indexing. Memory-o-matic [17] is such a detailed system. It provides for the cataloging and indexing of the preacher's library, the filing and indexing of all other kinds of materials. By its use a man can find material in his library dealing with any subject or text being studied. The indexing is done under both subjects and texts.

Many students will not likely be able to depend on memory or a detailed method of filing and indexing. Such men need a simple and easily used method of filing and indexing, as well as for cataloging and indexing their libraries.

---

[17] Available through The Mount Vernon Foundation, Mt. Rainier, Maryland.

The Efficiency Filing System [18] by L. R. Elliott describes such a system for organizing the preacher's library and a simple system for indexing the material of the library and other material. It is an easily used filing system.

The Eureka Filing System [19] is an adaptation of the Wilson Index System. It provides for the filing and indexing of loose materials, the indexing of books and periodicals, and the filing and indexing of sermons under subjects and texts. It is relatively simple and easily used.

Baker's Textual and Topical Filing System [20] by Neal Punt provides for the organizing of material in the preacher's library and filing cabinet by means of one complete index. The material is indexed under topics and texts. The grouping of material is practical, and the indexing is cross-referenced to avoid duplication. It is an easily used and readily expanded system of filing and indexing.

The Rossin-Dewey system [21] outlines a method for filing clippings, tracts, notes, and sermons by the use of the Dewey Decimal system of classification. It provides for grouping of similar materials and for cross-indexing. It is relatively simple to use, and its use of the Dewey Decimal system of classification correlates the preacher's filing with most public libraries.

A Word Fitly Spoken by Robert J. Hastings describes nearly forty sources of illustrations and gives examples. It also offers a system for classifying and filing them. [22]

The choice of a system of filing and indexing is an individual and personal matter, but some method should be adopted and used. It will enable the preacher to preserve his valuable material and will save him untold hours in time and energy.

---

[18] Nashville: Broadman Press, 1959, p. 81.

[19] Available through the Student Center, Southern Baptist Theological Seminary, Louisville, Kentucky.

[20] Grand Rapids: Baker Book House, 1960.

[21] Described in Donald F. Rossin and Palmer Ruschke, *Practical Study Methods for Student and Pastor* (2d ed.; Minneapolis: Donald F. Rossin Co., Inc., 1961).

[22] Nashville: Broadman Press, 1962.

V

Maturing the Idea

A growing idea which will produce a mature sermon is a priceless possession. Slowly and tediously this pearl of great price must be cultivated. Having an idea which ignites the sermon process, understanding God's Word as it bears on the sermon idea, and acquiring an abundance of materials to illume this idea are not sufficient in themselves. The preacher must let the originating idea, light from God's Word, and relevant materials live in his mind and possess his life until they represent the deepest conviction of his soul. These sermonic building blocks should be possessions of the man of God until they are fully seasoned. Until the idea is mature, the preacher is not adequately prepared to complete his organization, to polish his sermon, or to deliver his message.

Why should growth and maturity be discussed? What difference does it make whether a preacher takes an idea and preaches it immediately or takes time to test and develop it? Look at some positive values which accrue to the minister who is patient and persistent in letting his ideas mature.

Concreteness and clarity develop.—Maturity of thought brings concrete details and clarity to preaching. To refer to an apple in particular is clearer than to talk about fruit in general. To describe the apple as a delicious red apple is even better. A brief word picture of a beautiful brown and white two-year-old collie is preferable to mentioning only that one has a big dog at home. As intimate knowledge develops about the idea at hand, concrete and specific details become possible. "Specifics" light up the understanding of both adults and children.

Errors diminish.—Quick judgment often results in shallow,

misguided opinions. There is no place for immature judgment
in the pulpit. The redemption of man is at stake, and the development of young Christians hangs in the balance. Insights that
develop in time will prevent hasty and erroneous statements.
Often mental stone bruises may be avoided when one does not
jump to hasty conclusions.

Freshness develops.—Often the preacher's first ideas are commonplace and trite. These first impressions should be recorded,
however, because only by putting them down can their weak-
nesses be discovered. Better to discover the barrenness of a
thought in the study than in the pulpit. As ideas are recorded
and the process of maturing begins, the creative and imaginative
faculties of the mind go to work discarding inferior ideas for
better ones. If this procedure is properly pursued in each sermon, the quality and appeal of the message will increase. Illustrations project themselves into the picture from all sides.
Freshness comes as the preacher states eternal truths with new
vigor and varied insights.

Vitality emerges.—Vitality is the capstone of all the values
which accrue in the process of growing an idea. A fairly concrete sermon idea could emerge clear, fresh, and free from
error, and still not penetrate the hearts of the hearers because
of an absence of power or force. Warmth and vitality are
essential and will emerge with the proper maturation. The
preacher who would have the priceless treasure of maturity
must grapple with God, probe the depths of his mind, and
pursue maturity of thought through creative patience.

Maturity Through Divine Leadership

From the instant the sermon idea originates, throughout each
step in preparation until the delivery itself, the preacher should
work with the conviction that God is inspiring, leading, and
overshadowing him. This conviction comes only when the
minister seeks earnestly to know God's mind. By the very act
of standing in the pulpit, the preacher declares that he is speaking for God. In the very nature of his role as minister he must

speak for God, or he is nothing more than an orator with an empty and vain message. It is sheer mockery to profess to speak for God without actually having God's leadership. In spite of any and all difficulties involved in really knowing God's will, the preacher must find it. When he does, he will experience the glorious excitement of speaking in the name of the Lord.

Assurances of Divine Leadership

A relevant idea.—When the preacher meets a specific human need, his sermon is relevant. Unless preaching is directed to human need it falls short of being true preaching. Human need is always specific: a seventeen-year-old red-headed boy without salvation; an attractive high school girl losing her moral way; a successful businessman being destroyed by alcohol; a cafe waitress deserted by her husband; a Sunday school teacher cold and careless about her devotional life; a college student distressed in mind about the uniqueness of the Christian faith; a young mother with cancer; a deacon refusing to be a good steward; or a father living in fear of losing his job. The minister must so preach as to reach the hearts of his people with a message from the Lord. Surely only God can know perfectly the hearts of people. When the preacher finds God's answer to human needs, he knows that his sermon ideas are relevant.

A biblical idea.—Basically and fundamentally the need to be met must be matched with an appropriate passage of Scripture. Biblical truth is eternal and pertinent to every age. Let God speak to modern man in his twentieth-century dilemmas. Donald Miller states that true preaching is impossible without God's Word.

It is my own high conviction that the only right a man has to stand in a pulpit before a gathered congregation of men and presume to declare the living word of the living God by which he creates eternal life in the souls of men and makes them members of the new Israel, is that he is making an honest effort to bear witness to what he has found in the Bible. . . . If we, therefore, would

speak to men *in the name of God,* which alone is true preaching, we
must speak out of the Bible.[1]

The pastor must be careful in his handling of the Scriptures to
be sure that the portion he uses really speaks to the issue at
hand. The more direct the relationship between the issue and
Scripture, the more spiritually helpful will be the results.

A dynamic idea.—Sermon ideas provoke various reactions in
the preacher's mind. Some ideas seem to be logically correct,
but they leave the preacher cold. Occasionally some idea will
inspire, thrill, and move the preacher's own heart. This one
must be preached. Boldly and dramatically this thought takes
possession of his soul. He feels that the people will be robbed
of a great blessing if they do not receive this message. This does
not mean that the preacher will be a proud man with a vain
message, but that he will have warm feelings about his ideas.
When this happens, the minister knows that his heart has found
the fundamental idea for his message. Even though his idea is
relevant, biblical, and logical, unless the preacher is moved in
heart and soul, the people will not be moved. Surely God will
so inspire and impress the preacher's heart emotionally that he
will know that a particular idea is the proper one.

A harmonious idea.—Is it possible for the minister to preach
a message which does not match his life? Can a herald of God
powerfully proclaim the totality of Christian stewardship and
cheat on his personal gifts to God? Can he humbly set out the
Christian's obligation in racial issues while he harbors hate in his
heart? It is possible for one to preach a message which does not
harmonize with his life, but the message surely will be ineffective. When the life and message of the preacher are harmonious, the assurance of divine benediction floods his soul.

Values of Divine Assurance

Several positive values ensue when the minister of God stands
in his pulpit confident that God has led in the sermonic process.

---
[1] *Fire in Thy Mouth*, pp. 41-42.

A sense of peace.—Every preacher needs a sense of peace as he faces the constant pressure of another sermon to be prepared and delivered. Many times he dreads the thought of another Sunday. There is seemingly no relief. Sundays, Wednesdays, revivals, banquets, civic clubs, church organizations clamor for sermons, addresses, devotionals, and pep talks. The task is staggering. Frustration is real.

When a pastor organizes his time and follows God's leadership, he will avoid many problems. As a message becomes fixed in mind and heart, and on paper, peace comes. The herald of God can go to his bed Saturday night without the strain of a divided mind. He has done his best; the message is ready. When he faces Sunday morning, he does so without a sense of panic or frustration. Before the assembled people, he has peace and satisfaction resulting from the sure knowledge of work well-planned and completed.

A sense of authority.—When God speaks and the minister hears and obeys, he can preach with authority. It is unlikely that an uncertain word could be spoken by a preacher who knows God has commanded him to speak. The prophet Amos heard God's message and preached with bold authority.

> Then answered Amos, and said to Amaziah, I was no prophet, neither was I a prophet's son; but I was a herdsman, and a dresser of sycomore-trees: and Jehovah took me from following the flock, and Jehovah said unto me, Go, prophesy unto my people Israel. Now therefore hear thou the word of Jehovah (Amos 7:14-16, ASV).

Nothing less than the authority with which Amos spoke will be sufficient for a herald of God standing in a modern pulpit.

A sense of boldness.—The endowment of authority from God produces boldness. A mere mortal dares to speak boldly in the name of God to other men! Incredible! But it is God's plan for preachers. It was so from the first:

> The next sabbath almost the whole city was gathered together to

hear the word of God. But when the Jews saw the multitudes, they were filled with jealousy, and contradicted the things which were spoken by Paul, and blasphemed. And Paul and Barnabas spake out boldly, and said, It was necessary that the word of God should first be spoken to you (Acts 13:44-46, ASV).

Whether the Word be preached in the face of great difficulties or before a congregation of devout believers, the minister must proclaim it boldly. Stanley High relates this interesting story:

Someone once wrote Billy Graham: "Why is it you try to impose your views on others? How can you be sure? You are making the same mistake Jesus made."

So far as the last sentence is concerned, the propagation of "the mistake that Jesus made" is, I think, Billy Graham's life work. As for imposing his views, he often says, "This isn't my message. I'm only the messenger boy. I can't decide what you do about the message when you get it. I can only try to make sure you get it." And few phrases are repeated oftener in his sermons than these: "I didn't say it; Jesus said it." "This is not man's opinion; this is God's opinion." "It's not important what Billy Graham says; here is what the Bible says." [2]

Billy Graham is a bold preacher because he knows that God's hand is upon him and that God's words are in his mouth. A conviction such as this produces boldness.

Boldness is not arrogance, in spirit or in word. It is a fearlessness of character and speech which asserts itself in the name of the Lord. When the minister knows that he has God's leadership and, as a consequence, authority from on high, he then possesses boldness for effective preaching.

A sense of urgency.—Since the preacher has a message from God, based on his Word, and addressed to the needs of men, he will feel a sense of urgency about its delivery. Is it likely that

---

[2] *Billy Graham: The Personal Story of the Man, His Message, and His Mission* (New York: McGraw-Hill Book Co., Inc., 1956), p. 33.

a messenger bearing a crucial letter from the President of the United States to the United Nations would be lackadaisical in delivering it? Could a soldier bearing a vital message from his commanding general afford to be dilatory in the execution of his mission? Neither would a God-led preacher speak with anything but compelling urgency when carrying out the commands of the Lord. This does not mean that he will have a "seizure" in the pulpit, but that he will be emotionally involved in his task. Power from God comes not by a raving manner of speech, a pounding of the pulpit, or physical gymnastics on the platform. God's power comes, and the preacher will demonstrate by the urgency of his speech and conduct that he bears a message from the King.

Maturing Ideas in the Subconscious

An important step in the maturation of a sermonic idea is the probing of one's mind for related ideas and experiences. Not only does the conscious area of the mind contribute to maturation, but the subconscious mind must also be allowed to call out a vast treasure of experience which may be used to enrich the lives of others. This subconscious is better utilized than understood. Students of the human mind admit difficulty in understanding it and in agreeing on uniform terminology, but they do agree that it exists.

Students of the human mind are convinced we have two intimately related minds: The conscious mind and the subconscious, or unconscious or subliminal, mind. The brain consists of ten thousand million cells that rest neither day nor night. Only a part of the time, however, are we aware of what is going on in our brains. Some of our best thoughts, ideas, and insights flash into our conscious minds suddenly and spontaneously from our subconscious minds.[3]

Impressions made on the mind are not lost. The multiplicity

[3] Ilion T. Jones, *Principles and Practice of Preaching* (New York: Abingdon Press, 1956), p. 125.

of ideas and experiences that have been a part of a person's life are still a part of his being. They are stored in the subconscious. This fact, then, offers a creative challenge to the preacher to utilize a vast and mostly untapped storehouse for preaching.

A Planned Association of Ideas

By a deliberate turning of thought back into the subconscious, the preacher can search out and discover many experiences related to the idea he is maturing for pulpit use. For example, if he is in need of ideas relating to a joyful experience, he might, as he sits at his desk, recall a childhood visit to his grandmother. Flooding into his conscious mind from the subconscious would come vivid views of a ride down a hot, sandy, country lane, luscious red apples picked from the tree, homemade peach ice cream, fried chicken, hot country sausage, a cool nap on the front porch, and a long ride home after dark.

Or, if the preacher seeks an experience about discipline with love, he might recall the time when he at ten years of age helped his father burn autumn leaves. Picturesque and painful details troop into his conscious mind: raking red, brown, and yellow leaves; growing weary after fifteen minutes of work; throwing dirt on the fire; ignoring a command to stop playing and start raking; dashing for freedom from father (an "old" man of thirty-five); being captured before the street was crossed; and hearing the inevitable, "This hurts me more than it does you."

Regardless of the theme in the mind of the preacher, he can by concentration call out of the past the choicest experiences of his life. These do not smell of books and research, but of joy, sorrow, happiness—of life itself.

A Relaxed Association of Ideas

The relaxed method is closely related to the concentrated method, but it is different in that a free and relaxed association of ideas is the goal. The mind can not hold in immediate awareness all that it has experienced.

Let us suppose that this is a diagram of our mental state [see FIGURE 1]. The point "A" is the peak of consciousness. "B" is the subconscious. The small space above the dotted line contains all the conscious thoughts now available. That which is below, immense in any person, contains all the experiences one has ever had in life. Consciousness is little more than a point above the subconsciousness. If by any means the preacher could lower this level, represented by the dotted line, so that it would include material not usually available, he might secure illustrations and ideas which would materially assist him in the sermon.[4]

FIGURE 1   FIGURE 2   FIGURE 3

One must focus attention on the theme at hand and then lower that theme into the area of the mind which is below the conscious.

For instance, intense thinking focuses the mind on the subject, narrowing the conscious thought to nearly a point, thus [see FIGURE 2]. Then, by physical and mental relaxation, dropping off almost into sleep, yet refraining from sleep, the conscious level is suddenly but gently lowered, thus [see FIGURE 3].[5]

The mind is permitted to roam at will with its own experiences. In the millions of brain cells where experiences, incidents, events, thoughts, tragedies, sorrows, happinesses, and ideas unlimited are stored, the planted idea searches for and locates compatible thoughts which will immeasurably enrich itself.

A Delayed Association of Ideas

When the mind becomes tired and clogged from too much study and concentration, and when creative development appears to ebb, it is advisable to defer further mental probing and go about other tasks. In the doing of other work the mind is

---

[4] Bryan, *op. cit.*, p. 161.
[5] *Ibid.*

often liberated from its congestion. No attempt to force ideas to come should be made as other tasks are pursued. The idea must rest.

Every preacher has a dozen urgent things to care for at almost any moment. There are always sick people in hospitals, new people in the community to visit, a committee to call, a sorrowing family to comfort, teachers to enlist, errands to run, and countless other tasks to be done. When the mind ceases to be productive and creative in sermon preparation, the preacher might well be about other phases of kingdom business. He need not continue knocking on a gate that will not open. In due time the subconscious will toss out of the richness of its depth the very perspective that is being sought. Occasionally the brightest and most thrilling ideas will come at moments unexpected.

The unconscious mind apparently does not originate ideas but only works on what is prepared for it and handed to it by the conscious mind. Men do not suddenly discover bright ideas without reference to what they have been thinking previously. A flash of inspiration from the subconscious mind follows a period of hard work, of deep, vital concern about, and devotion to, a problem on the part of the conscious mind. But unquestionably the subconscious mind takes the seed thoughts that sink down into it from the conscious mind, assimilates and fuses them, and comes forth with a result which the conscious mind alone cannot produce.[6]

The preacher should always be ready to record in a notebook or on paper any flashes of inspiration that come from the subconscious. These flashes are gone in a moment and all that remains is the ghost of a vital and beautiful thought that is no more. Agony of soul befalls the minister who fails to capture these treasures prepared for but not recorded.

There seems to be no question but that God is responsible for many of the associations and relationships that well up from the subconscious.

---

[6] Jones, *op. cit.*, p. 126.

This "spiritual" explanation, of course, is not strange to Christian preachers, for they have always believed the Holy Spirit to be the source of their finest insights, inspirations, and illuminations. There is no reason why we may not believe our subconscious minds to be the channels through which the vital thoughts of God "get through" to us. By whatever means one tries to explain it, he will be wise to believe that God can do for his sermon what he alone cannot do. Those who have believed this have discovered what has been called "psychic power in preaching." But always remember that these "uprushes from the subliminal" come only when we have done our conscious work well.[7]

Creative sermon preparation is a difficult task. The minister who follows God's leadership and makes full use of life's experiences as the Holy Spirit directs will enrich his preaching.

Maturity Through the Creative Use of Time

Growth of the sermon idea does not take place automatically —merely by the passage of time. Numerous creative activities are necessary to promote growth.

Periodic Review

Some type of periodic review of sermon starters is essential. Many preachers have found invaluable a growing file of sermon ideas or sermon starters. How to keep them is not as important as the fact of keeping them. With one minister the process is detailed and elaborate and a well-organized file cabinet serves his sermonic needs. Another will simply drop into a drawer scraps of paper, half sheets, or whatever he has available for notes. Others use a notebook, clipboard, or folder for storing. Whatever the method of getting the material on paper and into some receptacle, a process of periodic review should always follow. Diligently and regularly the preacher should go through his collection of materials; once a week is not too often if the ideas are to develop and mature.

_____
[7] *Ibid.*, p. 127.

By this constant process of review and inspection the inventory of ideas is kept fresh and alive in the mind of the preacher. Furthermore, the very act of regularly inspecting these materials causes them to grow. As the preacher comes back again and again to a seed planted, he will discover that it has germinated, broken ground, and become a fruitful plant.

Creative Study

Through creative study—reading and research—the minister is able to add new dimensions of thought to his sermon idea. The preacher who knows little or nothing about a subject or the one who perceives only one or two facets of truth about it will have extreme difficulty in dividing, arranging, and organizing his material. When new perspectives are added through study, it is much easier to divide, arrange, and organize. If the preacher has clearly in mind only two facets of his idea, he can arrange them in only two ways: I–II or II–I. But if he has even as few as three facets, he will have six arrangements available to him:

1.	I	II	III	4. I	III	II
2.	II	III	I	5. II	I	III
3.	III	I	II	6. III	II	I

If there be four facets of knowledge about the basic idea, there are then twenty-four possible arrangements. The diligent minister does not suffer from a paucity of materials but deals with the delightful problem of the best way to arrange his choice thoughts. The burden is not then to have something to say, but to find the most felicitous method of arranging and saying it.

Homiletic Discussion

An idea prayed for, read and studied about, thought about, and generously discussed tends to develop and grow. Phillips Brooks each Monday morning followed the practice of inviting his friends, the Clericus Club, into his study for the express purpose of having the group mull over and discuss great ideas. These friends were not always aware that they were consider-

ing a sermon idea for Brooks, but nevertheless they greatly
contributed to the richness of his preaching. Such a program is
invaluable. The minister has various opportunities for discussing
his idea with both laymen and ministerial friends. A planned
Clericus Club after the pattern of Brooks would be profitable.

Pastoral Work

The essential pastoral work which a minister must perform
can become one of the most fruitful sources of ideas for preaching if, instead of allowing it to be merely an interruption of his
sermon preparation, he uses it. Study, reviews, and discussions
will be impotent at times to unlock the door to the sermon.
Calls in homes, hospitals, and places of business can often cast
a ray of light into a dark corner and supply the very facts
sought. A propitious idea speaks to numberless pastoral problems, and these problems in turn enrich the idea. A pastoral
call, while an idea is growing, will speak to the heart of the
preacher and generate new perspectives.

Devotional Life

Growth of the sermon idea is often limited by the little time
which the herald of God devotes to prayer, Bible reading,
meditation, and soul-searching. There is a positive and direct
ratio between depth of devotional life and richness of preaching. This cannot be faked or counterfeited. The people surely
know when their pastor has been with Jesus. As the coming
sermon is carried to the Lord daily, devotional growth occurs.
It is impossible to lay an idea before the Lord daily without the
idea growing in meaning and power.

In general, there are three ways to insure the growth or maturity of the sermon idea: first, by seeking divine leadership;
second, by allowing the subconscious to work; and third, by
using time creatively.

VI

Formulating the Structure

Form and content are vitally related in any piece of writing. When they are correctly matched, they are so harmonious as to be virtually inseparable. Like an architect planning and building a house, the preacher plans and builds his sermon so that his message attains a perfect blending of form and content. He develops his original sermon idea by relating it to a text, a thesis, and a specific objective. With these as starting materials he continues to plan for his sermon structure by interpreting the text, gathering additional materials, maturing his thought, and coming at last to the actual construction of his message—including title, introduction, body, conclusion, and invitation.

The Title

A much neglected aspect of sermon preparation is the title or stated name of the sermon. Even if the minister does not attach a formal name to his discussion, the message still develops some theme, general subject, or idea. When that idea is condensed into specific terms, it is the title.

The final form or statement of the title may crystallize at any step in sermon preparation. Whether the final form comes early or late in the preparation, the preacher will invariably have a general idea of his title almost from the beginning. Whenever this general idea of the title takes shape, the preacher should record it for guidance throughout sermon construction.

Values of the Title

A title, well phrased and precisely stated, enables the audience to understand clearly the intent of the preacher. It is remarkable that the preacher is the only person in the world of communication who tries constantly to communicate with people without telling them what it is he wants to communicate. A publisher would not think of sending out a book without a title any more than he would think of sending out a book without his name. The publishers of magazines not only entitle the magazines but also the articles within the magazines. Newspaper publishers give titles to their newspapers as well as captions to news stories. Movie producers expend great labor on the wording of movie titles. It seems strange that in the realm of preaching the principle of sharing with the audience the title under construction sometimes breaks down.

An effective title furnishes the preacher a divisible whole from which he can develop the framework of the sermon body. Even a general idea of the title helps the preacher in collecting, selecting, and condensing materials. A precise title is an invaluable tool in limiting and unifying each and every item in the structural development of the sermon. When a title has been well prepared, it is a guide which assists the preacher in sticking to the topic from introduction to invitation.

Essential Qualities for the Title

Clarity.—The title should be clear in wording. It should not be a mere listing of the sermon points from the body nor a revelation of everything to be covered in the sermon. Clarity is better secured by a lucid and concise group of words than by a summary of the body points.

Accuracy.—The title should be an accurate formulation of the content or purpose of the sermon. If one desires to discuss "The Values of Tithing," he should, in his presentation, show the values which accrue to the faithful Christian steward. It would be inappropriate with this title to spend fifteen to twenty minutes answering objections to tithing and five to seven minutes actually showing values. Having stated that he is going to preach on "The Values of Tithing," the preacher must discuss values. If he desires to preach on "Objections to Tithing," he should make his purpose clear in the title and stay with it.

Narrowness.—The title should be limited or restricted in scope. It would be rather difficult to discuss "God, the Universe, and Other Things" in a thirty-minute message. The title should be narrowed until it can be handled within the time limit. The title should also be limited to the topic with which the preacher is competent to deal. If, for example, one is not certain of "the fate of the heathen," he should not announce that as a title. Speculation confuses rather than instructs.

Brevity.—The title should be of manageable size, approximately two to seven words with not more than three or four strong words. One-word titles are too general in scope, while lengthy titles are burdensome, both to the preacher and to the audience.

Suitability.—The title should be phrased in terms appropriate and suitable for pulpit use. While political, economic, and ethical issues are of vital concern to the modern congregation, they should be distinctively related to the Christian message. While "Vital Relationship with Russia" and "Will the United States Use the Atomic Bomb on the Civilian Population?" are concerned with moral and ethical issues, they are typical of inappropriate political and secular headings.

In attempting to phrase a religious topic, it is neither necessary nor desirable to use a Scripture phrase as the title. It is far better to write into the title one's own interpretation of a text than to quote verbatim some part of the passage.

Relevancy.—The title should be relevant or vital to the needs of the people. The minister, through a personal knowledge and understanding of congregational needs, can fashion titles which will be of earnest concern—titles which will "make a difference."

Originality.—The title should be phrased in a fresh, interesting, and appealing way. Rarely does a felicitous title come immediately to a preacher. There is no easy road to securing pleasing titles. Even when one labors constantly and diligently, success is not always assured. However, brilliant and striking titles are well worth the effort they require.

The appealing title must not be confused with the cheap
sensational title. Some examples of the latter are: "If You Pull a
Bear's Tail, You Are Bound to Get Bit," "Charlie McCarthy
or Jesus Christ," "Why Every Preacher Should Go to Hell,"
"The Man Who Wouldn't Leave Women Alone," "Sausages
and Souls," "A Nudist in a Graveyard," "The Baptist Preacher
Who Lost His Head at a Dance," "Be Sharp for God," "Why
God Is Like a Hot Water Bottle," "The Man, the Woman, and
the Hotel Room," "Kissing in the Dark," "Painted Dog Meat,"
and "Drive Like Hell and You Will Soon Get There."

Sensational titles are irreverent, cheap, vulgar, and often sex-
ually suggestive. They reveal that the preacher has a low
estimate of his people, that he depends on gimmicks rather
than on spiritual power and biblical preaching, and that he
unashamedly parades a gospel adorned in cheap clothes before
sinful men.

In order to phrase an attractive title, it is not necessary to
strain for rhyme, rhythm, and alliteration. These elements may
be desirable and add interest, however, when they are natural
and logical.

Phrasing the Title

Phrasing a striking title is a vitally important part of sermon
preparation, but at the same time it is an extremely difficult
part. Some ministers seem to be gifted with the ability to "turn
a beautiful phrase," while most preachers must plod a rather
pedestrian path. The gifted minister needs little aid in developing skill in preparing titles, but the average preacher needs all
the assistance he can get.

One of the most useful procedures for constructing effective
titles has been described by R. C. H. Lenski.[1] He points out
that the title is intended to serve as an expression of the unity
of the sermon and that this unity should always be stated in a

---

[1] *The Sermon: Its Homiletical Construction* (Fort Worth, Texas: Potter's
Book Store, 1927). Many ideas, arrangements, and classifications have been
drawn from this most useful volume.

way that the title can be divided. Knowing that the title is to be divided, the preacher from the inception of the sermon will take proper steps to place a divisible element in the title. It is a waste of time and energy to formulate a poor title and then to spend hours trying to divide the indivisible. Divisible titles seldom happen by accident, but they can be perfected by work and practice.

A divisible title may be achieved by the inclusion of directional, clue, or arrow words, or phrases which point out the line of direction or indicate a key as to the divisions which will be delineated in the body. The key or line of direction may be accomplished by one of several ways: the emphatic word, the interrogative sentence, the imperative sentence, the declarative sentence, and the limiting word.

The emphatic word type line of direction.—The most popular and prevalent title is that which employs the emphatic word type line of direction. This title is constructed by placing the sermon idea in phrasal form. In the phrase one or two words, usually nouns, are arranged so as to receive major emphasis. It is around these major or emphatic words that the structural development of the sermon body gathers. In the following examples the emphatic or key word is italicized:

Title: "The *Habit* of Thankfulness" [2]
Text: 1 Thessalonians 5:18
         "In every thing give thanks: . . ."
Title: "The *Adequacy* of Christ." [3]
Text: Romans 10:11
         "For the scripture saith, Whosoever believeth
         on him shall not be put to shame."
Title: "The *Virtue* of Compassion" [4]

[2] John A. Broadus, *Sermons and Addresses* (Baltimore: H. M. Wharton & Co., 1886), pp. 45-56.
[3] George W. Truett, *Sermons from Paul,* ed. Powhatan W. James (Nashville: Broadman Press, 1947), pp. 35-45.
[4] Willard L. Sperry, *Sermons Preached at Harvard* (New York: Harper & Bros., 1953), pp. 45-53.

Text: Job 16:4
        "I also could speak as ye do: if your soul were
        in my soul's stead."

Title: "The *Appetite* of Iniquity" [5]
Text: Psalm 14:4, ASV
        "Have all the workers of iniquity no knowl-
            edge,
        Who eat up my people as they eat bread,
        And call not upon Jehovah?"

The interrogative sentence type line of direction.—The title
stated as a question is another popular method of establishing a
line of direction. The directional word in a question title is
either the interrogative word of the verb or verb phrase. In the
development of this form, the points of the sermon must answer
the question raised in the title. Therefore, questions which cannot be answered and trite questions with obvious answers
should be avoided.

The following titles by outstanding preachers illustrate the
interrogative sentence type line of direction:

Title: "*How* May We Know Jesus Better?" [6]
Text: Philippians 3:10
        "That I may know him . . ."

Title: "But When Life Tumbles In, *What* Then?" [7]
Text: Jeremiah 12:5
        "If thou hast run with the footmen, and they
        have wearied thee, then how canst thou con-
        tend with horses? and if in the land of peace,
        wherein thou trustedst, they wearied thee,
        then how wilt thou do in the swelling of
        Jordan?"

[5] Harold A. Bosley, *Sermons on the Psalms* (New York: Harper & Bros., 1956), pp. 24-35.
[6] George W. Truett, *A Quest for Souls,* comp. & ed. by J. B. Cranfill (Nashville: Broadman Press, 1917), pp. 290-302.
[7] Arthur John Gossip, "But When Life Tumbles In, What Then?" in *The Protestant Pulpit,* comp. Andrew W. Blackwood (New York: Abingdon Press, 1947), pp. 198-204.

Title: *"Can* We *Make* Sure of Tomorrow?" [8]
Text: Isaiah 56:12
        "To morrow shall be as this day, and much
        more abundant."

The imperative sentence type line of direction.—The line of
direction may be expressed by phrasing the title as an imperative sentence, indicating either a command or request. In this,
probably the rarest form of sermon titles, the discussion develops the command stated in the title. The verb is the arrow word.

Title: *"Be Born* Again in Christ!" [9]
Text: John 3:5-7
        "Jesus answered, Verily, verily, I say unto
        thee, Except a man be born of water and of the
        Spirit, he cannot enter into the kingdom of
        God. That which is born of the flesh is flesh;
        and that which is born of the Spirit is spirit.
        Marvel not that I say unto thee, Ye must be
        born again."

Title: "America, *Build* with the Bible!" [10]
Text: 2 Chronicles 17:9-10
        "And they taught in Judah, and had the book
        of the law of the Lord with them, and went
        about throughout all the cities of Judah, and
        taught the people. And the fear of the Lord
        fell upon all the kingdoms of the lands that
        were round about Judah, so that they made
        no war against Jehoshaphat."

Title: *"Pick* the Right Ancestors" [11]
Text: Psalm 16:6
        "The lines are fallen unto me in pleasant places;
        yea, I have a goodly heritage."

[8] Alexander Maclaren, *The Secret of Power and Other Sermons* (New York: Funk & Wagnalls Co., 1905), pp. 187-200.

[9] Walter A. Maier, *Let Us Return unto the Lord* (St. Louis: Concordia Publishing House, 1947), pp. 37-52.

[10] *Ibid.*, pp. 165-83.

[11] Bosley, *op. cit.*, pp. 36-48.

The declarative sentence type line of direction.—Another rare title form is that which indicates the line of direction by means of the declarative sentence. In this statement or assertion the body development deals with the affirmation set out in the title. The arrow word in the declarative sentence title is again the verb.

Title: "Life *Is* an Echo." [12]
Text: Matthew 7:2
        "With what measure ye mete, it shall be measured to you again."

Title: "Life *Demands* Loyalties" [13]
Text: Psalm 27:1-14, ASV
        "Jehovah is my light and my salvation;
        Whom shall I fear?
        Jehovah is the strength of my life;
        Of whom shall I be afraid?"

Title: "Truth *Is* the Banner" [14]
Text: Psalms 60:1-4; 61:1-8
        ". . . Thou has given a banner to them that fear thee, that it may be displayed because of the truth . . ."

The limiting word type line of direction.—The line of direction is sometimes established by adding modifiers or limiting words to the title. For example, "Love," a title too comprehensive in itself, may be limited like this: "God's Love." Though the title has been narrowed and has begun to take shape, it is still too broad. Other modifiers should be added to give it more precise shading, as for example: "God's Love to Fallen Man." [15] The word *love* should be modified or pointed in a particular direction, according to the text and the purpose

[12] C. Roy Angell, *Iron Shoes* (Nashville: Broadman Press, 1953), pp. 36-43.
[13] Bosley, *op. cit.*, pp. 59-68.
[14] *Ibid.*, pp. 78-86.
[15] John Wesley, "God's Love to Fallen Man," in *Sunday Half Hours with Great Preachers*, ed. Jesse Lyman Hurlbut (Philadelphia: John C. Winston Co., 1907), pp. 170-80.

of the preacher. Sometimes the addition of even one word to a
title improves the title immeasurably.

The arrow or distinctive word is the primary modifier in the
title and usually answers one of the following questions:
Which? How many? What kind? Whose? When? Where?
Why? How? How often? How much?

Title: "The *Second* Mile" [16] (Which?)
Text: Matthew 5:41
         "Whosoever shall compel thee to go a mile,
         go with him twain."

Title: "The *Second* Coming of Christ" [17] (Which?)
Text: Revelation 22:20
         "Surely I come quickly. Amen. Even so,
         come, Lord Jesus."

Title: "The *One Sufficient* Refuge" [18] (How many?
         What kind?)
Text: Psalm 142:4-5
         "Refuge failed me . . . I cried unto thee, O
         Lord: I said, Thou art my refuge."

Title: "The *Sinner's* Surrender to His Preserver" [19]
         (Whose?)
Text: Job 7:20
         "I have sinned; what shall I do unto thee, O
         thou preserver of men?"

Title: "*Love's* Triumph Over Sin" [20] (Whose?)
Text: Mark 16:7
         "Tell his disciples and Peter that he goeth
         before you into Galilee."

---

[16] Angell, *op. cit.*, pp. 94-105.

[17] J. B. Cranfill (comp.), *Sermons and Life Sketch of B. H. Carroll* (Phila-delphia: American Baptist Publication Society, 1893), pp. 382-95.

[18] Truett, *A Quest for Souls*, pp. 338-58.

[19] Charles H. Spurgeon, *My Sermon Notes: A Selection from Outlines of Discourses Delivered at the Metropolitan Tabernacle* (New York: Funk & Wagnalls Co., 1884), I, pp. 181-84.

[20] Alexander Maclaren, *Sermons Preached in Manchester* (Second Series: New York: Funk & Wagnalls Co., 1905), pp. 58-70.

Title: "*God's* Help in the Hour of Trial" [21]
        (Whose?)
Text   Revelation 3:10
        "Because thou hast kept the word of my pa-
        tience, I also will keep thee from the hour of
        temptation."

Title: "*Larger* Ideas of God" [22] (What kind?)
Text: Isaiah 28:20
        "For the bed is shorter than a man can stretch
        himself on it: and the covering narrower than
        that he can wrap himself in it."

Title: "*When* Jesus Comes to Our Town" [23] (When?)
Text: Matthew 21:10
        "And when he was come into Jerusalem, all
        the city was moved, saying, Who is this?"

Title: "The *Strangest* Place" [24] (What kind?)
Text: Matthew 2:15
        "Out of Egypt have I called my son."

Title: "The *Best* Friend" [25] (Which?)
Text: Proverbs 27:10
        "Thine own friend, and thy father's friend,
        forsake not."

Announcing the Title

That the congregation may clearly understand the idea to
be communicated, the preacher should orally present the title
in some direct or indirect manner. The logical place for the
statement of the title is within the introduction. On rare occasions, perhaps for the purpose of holding attention, the preacher
may desire to state the title in the conclusion.

[21] B. H. Carroll, *Evangelistic Sermons*, comp. J. B. Cranfill (New York: Fleming H. Revell Co., 1913), pp. 163-82.

[22] Sperry, *op. cit.*, pp. 37-44.

[23] Leslie R. Marston, "When Jesus Comes to Our Town," in *Special-Day Sermons for Evangelicals*, comp. & ed. Andrew W. Blackwood (Great Neck, N.Y.: Channel Press, Inc., 1961), pp. 115-26.

[24] Eugene Carson Blake, "The Strangest Place," in Macleod, *op. cit.*, pp. 27-34.

[25] Spurgeon, *My Sermon Notes*, pp. 287-90.

Various approaches may be used to present the title. One may begin with a direct statement: "My title is 'The Cost of Discipleship.'" He may prefer to say: "Mark 8:27 to 9:1 makes clear 'The Cost of Discipleship'"; or "In our initial service together in this week of daily meetings, let us think together on 'The Cost of Discipleship.'" Other suggestions for announcing the title are: "The text suggests this thought for our consideration . . ."; "The title for the morning is . . ."; "For our consideration I present the title . . ." It makes little difference whether the title is announced directly or indirectly so long as the congregation understands what idea is to be considered.

The Body

The sermon has three major structural parts: introduction, body, and conclusion. The order of preparation of these three is: first, the body; second, the conclusion; and third, the introduction.

Outlining the Body

Principles of organization.—A carefully written outline of the body of the sermon furnishes the preacher a basic plan or framework to give order and arrangement to ideas that would otherwise be confused. From a mass of details arising from general study, important points should be isolated, arranged in logical order, and given the emphasis they deserve. Outlining the title—as it embodies the thesis, goal, and text—is the quickest and easiest way to plan what is to be said. It also helps in grouping sentences into paragraphs to show the readers or listeners what the main points are and aid them in understanding what is being said.

The preacher may begin an outline by jotting down all the points or ideas that seem important or all that he wants to include in the sermon. He should then study the list to see which items are related, which items are similar or different, and which items seem unrelated to the rest.

After carefully considering the items, the sermon-builder

should rearrange the points, grouping related ideas together under a main point. Attention should then be given to the main points to determine which of these are of major importance and which are only details. Each detail should then be written under the major point to which it refers or discarded if it seems not to fit anywhere.

The order in which the main points will be presented must then be decided. There follows the arrangement of details under each main heading. These major and minor points are then ready to be put into a working outline as main topics and sub-topics. The main topics are numbered I, II, III, with the sub-topics under each indented and numbered 1, 2, 3 (or as some prefer A, B, C). Further subtopics, if *needed*, are indented and numbered (1), (2), (3). Two orders—topics and subtopics—are generally sufficient.

To master the principles of outlining, it is helpful to follow several important guides. (1) All major and minor points should be written in sentence or phrasal form. It is important that the form be parallel, *i.e.*, that all major topics be expressed similarly, and that all subheads be expressed in similar form. The phrasal and sentence structure should not be used together in the same outline. (2) Every point that is divided must have two or more parts. If there is only one subtopic it should be included in the larger topic. (3) Every subtopic should explain the point of which it is a division. (4) Illustrations are not numbered as divisions in the outline. (5) Scripture references are not numbered as divisions in the outline. (6) Sermon material, such as exegesis, argument, or application, which explains a point but does not divide it should not be numbered in the outline. (7) The terms introduction, body, conclusion, invitation should not be included in the outline since they are organizational items and not topics to be discussed in the sermon body. (8) No item of any rank should contain more than one concept or idea.

Patterns for organization.—In arranging the major headings and subtopics in a manageable order or sequence one of several patterns of organization may be followed. "There are two kinds of order, *natural order* and *logical order*. The natural orders, like the time sequence of events, are inherent in the material itself; the logical orders are imposed by the mind of the writer on material which, like weeds in a garden, might occur in any chance pattern or in none at all." [26]

The natural orders include the *order of time* and the *order of space*. These patterns of organization are derived from man's experience with the natural or physical world—the now and then, the up and down, the along and across.

In the *order of time* arrangement, time is the chief concern—when a thing happened or should happen. The events are presented in narrative form chronologically in the order in which they happen. In exposition the directions or steps in a process or procedure are listed from beginning to end. Main headings in the sermon might be arranged past, present, and future; or origin, development, and consummation. While the order of time is common, it is also one of the least interesting orders. Sometimes, however, it is essential. For example, in explaining the process of salvation, one should certainly use the order: repentance, faith, and confession. It is usually best, however, to choose an order other than time if another order seems to fit the nature of the sermon materials.

While *when* is of major importance in the order of time arrangement, *where* is of major importance in the *order of space*. Spatial organization is particularly useful in descriptive presentation. In it the points are described according to their location in a photograph—from foreground to background, from top to bottom, from side to side, from left to right, from front to back, from point to adjacent point in space. A sermon on the trials of Jesus, stressing the various locations of the trials, or a sermon on Christian love, stressing its length, breadth, depth, and height, utilize the order of space arrangement.

More effective than the natural orders of time and space are the *logical orders*. The logical orders include many types of

---

[26] Robert Hamilton Moore, *Effective Writing* (2nd ed.: New York: Holt, Rinehart & Winston, 1959), p. 78.

organization which are imposed on the sermon materials by the preacher's mind and which seem logical or reasonable to the preacher or to his hearers.

1. The main points of the outline may be arranged in the *order of importance* or the *order of climax*. Order of importance usually means that the items are arranged in an order of ascending importance from the least important items to the most important. Since the final position is the most emphatic, each new idea should be more important than the preceding. Climactic order may be profitable in presenting evidence in support of an opinion or argument. For example, the preacher, after stating his belief that all Christians should tithe, should give several reasons for his opinion, naming the least important first and the most important last. This device is capable of developing tremendous emotional appeal or a convincing intellectual attitude.

2. A logical order commonly used is the *order of general to specific*. In this pattern the preacher begins with broad generalizations or large classes before mentioning specific details and supporting statements or smaller groups and individuals. Time, space, and the position of the most important material is not of primary concern. The ideas are not necessarily arranged in a definite order of increasing or decreasing importance. In the general-to-specific order, sometimes known as deductive order, the thesis or controlling idea is presented first. The rest of the sermon then specifically supports that general statement. A deductive argument may be stated in the form of a syllogism, which contains three parts: (1) the major premise or generalization with which the argument begins; (2) the minor premise, or the particular situation to which the major premise is applied; (3) the conclusion. If the major and minor premise are true, if no significant fact has been ignored in the major premise, if the conclusion follows logically, the conclusion is likely to be sound. An unsound deductive conclusion is similar to a hasty generalization in inductive reasoning, for it may literally leap over or ignore significant facts in "jumping to conclusions."

3. The *specific-to-general order*, or inductive order, is less commonly used than its opposite, the general-to-specific order. In the inductive pattern the thesis or general truth is presented after specific instances have been presented one by one to lead up to the generalization. In the deductive order the thesis looks forward to the material that is to come; in the inductive order the thesis looks backward to the material already presented. The more evidence (facts, statistics, and other supporting materials) the preacher has in favor of a generalization, the more reliable the generalization is likely to become. He should be careful to avoid generalizations based on insufficient evidence. Hearsay, legend, mere opinion, or speculation also constitute insufficient evidence. A fact cited in support of a generalization must either be verified or attested by a reliable, unprejudiced, competent, up-to-date authority.

4. The *order of cause to effect* starts by naming a cause and tracing from it consequences or results. For example, one might begin with Jezebel's coveting of Naboth's vineyard and show how it resulted in the destruction of her and her husband and in the loss of the kingdom. This order is particularly applicable to historical sermons because chronological order is often used with it.

5. The *order of effect to cause* begins with the effect and attempts to discover the probable causes. It is used less frequently than the cause-to-effect order. In following this pattern of arrangement, care should be taken to avoid the mistake of assuming that because one event precedes another it is the cause of the second event.

6. The *order of question to answer* or the quiz approach employs the use of questions, stated in the major divisions of the sermon, with the answers developed in the subheadings. Using the title, "Crown Christ Your King," one might arrange the following outline:

      I.   Why should I crown him?

     II.   How should I crown him?

    III.   When should I crown him?

Caution should be exercised in using this pattern since sermons which are developed in this way tend to be uninteresting and to sound very much alike. Moreover, when the preacher announces a question for his first major division, the discerning members of his congregation will likely guess what his subsequent divisions are. A variation of the question-to-answer pattern—more interesting and hence more desirable—is the naming of answers to questions, asked in the preacher's mind but not explicitly stated to the congregation. In this order the title of the sermon is not in the form of a question but the preacher asks himself questions about the title. A sermon may answer one or more of the following questions as needed: Who? Whom? Whose? Which? What? When? Where? Why? How? Perhaps the preacher may choose to develop "Crown Christ Your King" by using only one question, "Why?" He could build his sermon with logical answers—divine birth, glorious life, vicarious death, thrilling resurrection, and present glorification. Or, if he desires, he could choose several questions and answer them without explicitly stating the questions.

CROWN CHRIST YOUR KING

I. He is worthy to be crowned. (Why?)
   Birth, life, death, resurrection, glorification
II. He is worthy to be crowned in every area of one's life. (Where?)
   In the home, in the school, on the job, in the inner life
III. He is worthy to be crowned now. (When?)

7. The *order of comparison and/or contrast* may be used when the preacher wishes to compare or contrast two persons, places, things, or ideas. According to his purpose, he may choose the order of comparison, in which he would show only similarities or likenesses, or the order of contrast, in which he would show only dissimilarities or differences. Details or reasons should be arranged in such a way as to bring out clearly the nature of either the comparison or the contrast.

One of two arrangements may be used in showing the similarities or dissimilarities: (1) details, reasons, or other basic materials supporting one view may be grouped together first, followed by a group of basic materials supporting the opposite point of view; (2) basic materials of similarity or difference may be compared or contrasted one by one.

Comparisons are useful in emphasizing a basic idea while contrasts are frequently used to show the superiority of one object, person, place, way of life, or idea over another. Comparisons or contrasts are often used in describing, explaining, or analyzing.

The once popular but now trite positive-negative pattern makes use of contrasts. In the first division a subject is treated from a positive standpoint and in the second division from the negative or opposite viewpoint or vice versa. Since the audience usually anticipates the second division when the first is announced, this treatment is not usually a desirable one.

The "yea-nay" pattern, though similar to the positive-negative in that it treats opposites, is superior to it. In this approach it is possible to state the first division without revealing what the second is. Although the audience may realize that a contrast is to be made, it is not aware of the nature of the contrast. Luccock discusses this pattern under the heading "twin sermons."

It may follow this form: (1) This statement is not true in one sense; but (2) it is true in another sense, usually a deeper or a broader one. . . .

Suppose the theme were God's gift of peace and the text, "My peace I give unto you." The progress might be along this line: (1) This is not true in a way commonly accepted and in a wrong idea of peaceful life—that of a placid, unruffled existence. If that is what you want, stay as far away from Christ as you can. He is the great upsetter; he brings "a sword"; he sets "at variance"; he breaks up the complacent self-satisfaction; etc.; But (2) it is true that Christ does bring a deep peace to the mind that is stayed on God. No matter what storms may sweep the surface. . . .[27]

---

[27] *Op. cit.,* pp. 140-41.

Sometimes the preacher's thesis may demand a pattern including both comparison and contrast. In using this combination, he may choose to group points of comparison first, followed by points of contrast, or he may prefer to show one point of likeness followed by one of difference. He will choose the arrangement which seems to him the most effective for the material.

In using the order of comparison or contrast, three things should be remembered: (1) When the order of comparison is followed, only materials that show how the things being compared are alike should be included. (2) When the order of contrast is followed, only the materials that show how the things being contrasted are alike should be included. (3) When an order of combined comparison and contrast is followed, materials pertaining to both should be included and arranged according to a definite plan of development.

8. The *order of analogy* may be followed if the preacher wants to suggest a similarity of relationship among sets of things, as believers relate to Christ and branches to the vine, or as the pastor serves his people and the shepherd serves his flock. The essential idea of relation is always found in good analogy. The analogy must show that the relation between certain things is like the relation between certain other things.

Even at the risk of seeming pedantic, the preacher should clearly reveal to his audience the fact that he is using analogy. By informing his hearers, he can keep them from misunderstanding the Scripture. If, for example, he shows how Noah's ark and God's plan of salvation in Noah's day are analogous to Christ and God's plan of salvation today, he should clearly enunciate his procedure lest those who hear equate Noah's ark and Christ as acceptable means of salvation.

Two points should be kept in mind when one follows the order of analogy. First, analogy never proves anything. Its usefulness lies in its ability to clarify meaning. Second, analogy becomes weaker and weaker the further it is carried. Since there are more dissimilarities than similarities, most analogies grow weaker the longer they are developed.

9. The *order of problem to solution* is also called life-situation preaching, a form of preaching brought to prominence by Fosdick in 1928. This order may be practiced in several ways.

In the *classification* sermon, possible attitudes and courses of conduct are explored. These may be general answers to the question, "What should I do?"

A typical form is that which points out different ways in which an issue can be met. How to meet trouble, for instance? Well, men have met it in three ways: Some have grown bitter. Others have "thrown up the sponge." Others have kept on going, upheld by a great faith. Here, for instance, is the way in which one man met great trouble: "We are troubled on every side, yet not distressed; we are perplexed, but not in despair; persecuted, but not forsaken; cast down, yet not destroyed." [28]

The *chase* [29] technique presents several possible solutions and proceeds in each division except the last to show each solution, one by one, inadequate or unsatisfactory. In the final division a satisfactory answer is found.

Occasionally only *partial* answers to a problem are given in each division. Some subjects are of such nature that several facets must be presented in order to see the whole solution. Each division is a part of the final solution and helps to form a composite answer.

The *case study* method affords an excellent opportunity for addressing a vital problem faced by different groups within the congregation. There are two approaches to the case study method. First, one might set out a problem and show a biblical case in which the issue was properly handled. Second, one might set out a problem with a solution and then by four, five, or six hypothetical cases show how the solution would work if applied in these cases. Phillips Brooks used the latter method effectively.

---

[28] Luccock, *op. cit.*, p. 138.
[29] *Ibid.*, p. 143.

In a sermon of this kind he would establish a principle, which he drew from the Scriptures; then he would show how the principle worked in the lives of Boston people, one after another, perhaps five or six in all. He did not merely turn to such examples as illustrations; he employed personal facts as building blocks in making the sermon.[30]

10. The *order of definition* is a useful and often essential pattern of development when the preacher wishes to clarify the meaning of something or to be sure that the listeners understand what he means by the words in the context in which he is using them. This pattern might begin with a simple dictionary definition, which nearly always includes placing the term in a general class and then pointing out how it differs from other things in that general class. An extended definition will help to clarify terms which people often interpret in different ways, unfamiliar or complex terms. An extended definition might analyze or divide a subject into its parts and discuss each part. The preacher might prefer to show what the term does not mean, or he might repeat or restate the meaning in different terminology. He may choose to trace the history or the development of the subject. He may prefer to use examples, comparisons, or contrasts.

For example, the preacher might raise the question, "What do you mean by *murder?*" He might then define it by placing it in the larger class to which it belongs—unlawful killing of a human being—and then show how it differs from other members of that class, suicide, for example. He might then discuss Jesus' interpretation of the Sixth Commandment against murder in Matthew 5:21-22:

Ye have heard that it was said of them of old times, Thou shalt not kill; and whosover shall kill shall be in danger of the judgment: but I say unto you, that every one who is angry with his brother shall be in danger of the judgment; and whosoever shall say to his

---

[30] Blackwood, *The Preparation of Sermons*, p. 146.

brother, Raca, shall be in danger of the council; and whosoever shall say, Thou fool, shall be in danger of the hell of fire (ASV).

Other interpretations, attitudes, examples, illustrations, or reasons may be included in this pattern of development, but every item used must contribute to the definition.

11. The *order of analysis*, though closely related to definition, is more than a mere method of definition. It includes breaking a subject or text into its parts, studying the parts separately, relating the parts to each other and to the whole. The analytical method may be used to develop anything that can be discussed by division into parts: the structure, the difficulties, the functions, the causes, the results, or the development of or the reasons for something.

12. The *order of acceptability* presents those ideas which are most likely to be pleasant or acceptable to the hearers before those which they might find unpleasant or unacceptable. It acknowledges the irrefutable points of an opponent's argument before refuting all the foolish things he has held.

The *ladder* pattern of arrangement utilizes the order of acceptability as it purposes to lead the congregation from acknowledgment or recognition of a truth to surrender to the truth, and to delight in the following of that truth. It progresses from point to point like the rungs of a ladder. Luccock quotes William James in *A Pluralistic Universe:*

On the first rung of the ladder we say of a momentous view of life, or of the world, or of religion, that it is a possible view, it is not self-contradictory, it is not absurd; on the second round we may say it *might* well be true as far as the actual facts are concerned; on the third we may say, it *may* be true now for all that anybody knows; on the fourth we add, it is *fit* to be true; on the fifth, it *ought* to be true; and on the sixth we affirm it *must* be true. Well, then, we say at the top of the ladder, it *shall* be true, at any rate for me, because I am going to adopt it as my truth and live by it henceforth.[31]

---

[31] *Op. cit.,* p. 136.

Lenski refers to this pattern of arrangement as "categories of possibility, actuality, and necessity."

Its mark is that of modality. That means, that an act, or a course of action, an achievement, a goal, or a result, may be viewed in various ways. We may picture it as a possibility, show it as an actuality, describe it as a necessity. Or, to put it more simply, we operate with these ideas: I must—I ought—I can—I will—I am privileged—I rejoice.

Take the idea of bearing the cross. It means suffering, it is hard, hence I may well face it by saying: I *must* bear the cross. Yet it also means spiritual benefit, honor from the Lord, so that I may well add: I *will* bear the cross. Then the cross leads to the crown, so that I may rise still higher: I *rejoice* to bear the cross. And the theme may be, "How the Christian Faces the Cross." [32]

The order of acceptability pattern is particularly suitable for argument, persuasion, and the appeal to reason.

13. The *order of dominant impression* is often used in descriptive sermons and is closely related to the order of general to specific. It gives first the general impression—saying something is "opinionated," "outmoded," "urbane"—before giving the basic materials which support the dominant impression and enable the listeners to visualize the object being described. Should a contradictory detail be important, it is entered as a striking contradiction of the dominant impression, emphasizing it by its very unexpectedness.

Closely related to the order of dominant impression is the *surprise-package* [33] type of arrangement in which the preacher develops a certain line of thought in the first division and then abruptly switches to a rather surprising idea in his second point. The second point must be a development of the topic. For example, in a sermon on "The Commandment to Love" from Mark 12:28-34, the minister might explore the principle of total love for God and neighbor as given by Christ. In the second

[32] *Op. cit.,* p. 99.
[33] Luccock, *op. cit.,* p. 142.

half of the message he might turn to the often ignored idea that love of neighbor is to be in the same degree as one loves himself.

The *order of psychological effect* or the *point of view*, more logical than the order of dominant impression, presents the material according to the way in which it would attract the attention of the beholder. Using terminology which appeals to one of the senses, the preacher arranges his materials from a particular point of view. He must put himself into the minds of the characters he discusses and must choose those details which the characters would be likely to choose. The order of psychological effect is especially useful in descriptive or narrative sermons.

A variation of this order is the *subjective-objective arrangement* point of view. In this approach the title is seen and examined from the viewpoint of the inner man or man's thoughts and from the viewpoint of the outer man or man's actions. "The Distress of a Christian" might be divided to show the anguish of a soul because of a lack of dedication to God, prayer, spiritual growth, and joy in the inner life, and the anguish of a soul because of a lack of service and concern for fellow man in his overt behavior toward others.

Another effective variation of the point of view is the *divine-human* arrangement which presents the topic from God's viewpoint and from man's viewpoint, or vice versa. For example, Lenski offers a two-point division of "The Glorious Easter Message of the Open Tomb" from Luke 24:1-12:

> I. What does it tell us about him who died?
> II. What does it tell us about who shall live?[34]

A similar approach is the *time and eternity* points of view. In this arrangement the subject is presented and examined as to how it looks now and how it will look at the consummation of the ages, or it is presented from the viewpoint of how it looks on earth and how it looks in heaven.

---

[34] *Op. cit.,* p. 93.

14. The *order of familiarity* begins with what the congregation knows and understands and moves to what is strange or unknown. The preacher might take advantage of this well-known principle of learning when he is presenting difficult concepts such as the kingdom of heaven (Matt. 13). In using analogies and parables he will also follow the order of familiarity.

15. The *order of utility* arranges the major divisions in the sequence in which they will be needed by the hearer to understand what is to follow. The partial answer type of arrangement takes advantage of the order of utility.

16. The *order of complexity* arranges the more simple material ahead of the more complicated. Basic elements are presented before puzzling exceptions.

Occasionally a sermon may be simple enough to require only one or two of the patterns of organization. More often one pattern governs the over-all organization of the sermon, and other patterns are used to guide the arrangement of details in individual sections or paragraphs. For example, a sermon might utilize the order of time pattern for its structural arrangement while individual sections might utilize the order of climax, the order of analysis, or whichever pattern seems most suitable for the material and would produce the most effective results. Several orders might also be superimposed in a single paragraph to produce a more complex effect than any one order alone can produce.

Developing the Body

The completion of the outline marks the close of the preparation or planning phase. There follows the writing step or the development of the body, which begins with the writing of a rough draft and ends with the writing of a final manuscript.

Using the outline as a guide, the sermon-builder should begin to write as rapidly and as freely as he can. At this point little attention is given to the technicalities of grammar, punctuation, spelling, and sentence structure. Since correcting errors tends to interrupt the flow of ideas, it should be postponed until the revision and polishing step. It is helpful to write the first draft in widely spaced lines, leaving room for correction.

As the preacher develops the outline, he will compose paragraphs contributing to the development of his central idea or thesis. He may use one paragraph to cover a point or subpoint, or he may use as many paragraphs as he needs to develop each point.

Each paragraph should have its own thesis which is usually expressed in a *topic sentence*. Like the whole sermon, each paragraph must be unified, treating only the idea contained in its topic sentence. Though the topic sentence may appear at any point in the paragraph, it is usually the first or the last sentence of the paragraph. Occasionally it is only implied. Most expository and argumentative paragraphs present their topic sentences explicitly while narrative and descriptive paragraphs frequently do not. Whether the topic sentence is expressed or implied, the preacher should make certain that every sentence contributes to the central idea of the paragraph, for only in this way does the paragraph achieve *unity*.

The preacher should also make sure that each topic sentence is developed fully, concretely, and specifically, leaving no questions unanswered. He should say all that he wants or needs to say about his point and all that the hearer needs to know. He may develop the topic sentence by the use of explanation (exegesis, analysis, definition), details, illustrations (anecdotes, incidents, facts, examples), arguments in a line of reasoning, comparisons or contrasts, application, or by a combination of these methods. Through an adequate development of the topic sentence the paragraph achieves *completeness*.

Careful attention to the organization of details within the paragraph is essential. The same patterns of the natural or logical orders which apply to the over-all sermon also apply to paragraphs. For example, the illustrations within a paragraph may be arranged according to the order of complexity, the order of climax, or any other order, depending on which pattern would be most effective. Arranging the ideas within a paragraph so that they are logically and clearly related to one another is one way of achieving *coherence.*

Coherence within the paragraph is based on the logical progression of thought from one sentence to another. When ideas are logically arranged, one or more of five literary devices may be employed:

1. Connectives: conjunctions (and, but, or, nor, for, because, if, unless, until); conjunctive adverbs (however, therefore, consequently, moreover, nevertheless, then, so, yet); transitional adverbs (similarly, contrarily, likewise, first, second, finally)
2. Transitional phrases: on the other hand, in addition, by the same token, at the same time, a few days later, so long as
3. Repetition of key terms
4. Pronouns looking back to antecedent nouns.
5. Repetition of sentence patterns

The use of these devices contributes to an easy flow of language which enables the hearers to understand clearly the intent of the preacher.

Not only must there be coherence within the paragraphs, but there must be coherence between paragraphs and between sections. Assuming that the ideas are logically arranged, the preacher may utilize one or more of the following devices to accomplish a smooth transition from one paragraph to the next.

1. Repetition of the last words in the preceding paragraph, word for word, or repetition of one or more key words from the preceding paragraph
2. Connective words
3. Transitional phrases
4. Pronouns looking back to antecedent nouns
5. Repetition of key terms

Regardless of the patterns and methods used, all sentences, paragraphs, and sections of the sermons must be bound into a coherent, fluent whole, noting all ideas and indicating explicitly their interrelations. Only then is the congregation free to give its best attention to the central idea the minister is presenting.

After the rough draft of the structural outline has been developed, a rough draft of the conclusion and introduction should be written. With the complete rough draft in hand, the preacher is ready to turn his attention to the important task of revision.

The Conclusion

The conclusion is that part of the sermon designed for the renewed emphasis on the *purpose* of the message. It states for a final time the *thesis* and *specific objective*. It is the preacher's last opportunity to impress his purpose upon the hearts of the hearers. Blackwood [35] believes that the conclusion surpasses in importance all items in the sermon except the text.

The finest skills available to the preacher should be used to insure that the conclusion accomplishes its high purpose. Worship through prayer, stewardship, singing, and Bible reading is over. The message has been almost completed and only a few moments remain. The crisis is at hand. The moment of decision has come. Furnishing an exacting target for the preacher, the conclusion is the time to bring all things to a harmonious and moving culmination. Because the message is now to come into sharpest focus, the conclusion is a time of suspense when not only the greatest opportunities but also the greatest dangers are present.

Careful planning of the conclusion will enable the preacher to avoid some common pitfalls. One pitfall, very disconcerting to the congregation, is the broken-promise conclusion, in which the preacher states repeatedly that he will presently conclude, or that with one more illustration he will finish the sermon, and yet he continues on and on. If this type of conclusion is compared to the pilot's landing of an airship, one might visualize the preacher's bringing the sermon-ship in for a landing and immediately taking off again.

---

[35] *The Preparation of Sermons*, p. 162.

An even more serious pitfall is the rambling conclusion, in which the preacher wanders aimlessly. He seems unable to land the sermon-ship and continues to circle the field until he runs out of gas. When he finally comes in for a landing, he is exhausted, the congregation is weary, and the clock is ticking toward 12:30 P.M.

The conclusion, like the introduction, varies in length according to the length of the entire sermon. As a general rule the conclusion should be brief, consuming about 10 per cent of the total time of delivery, but occasionally it may be longer or shorter.

Desirable Qualities of the Conclusion

In addition to the qualities of *unity*, *clarity*, and *coherence*, so essential to every part of the sermon, the conclusion should also be *personal*, *specific*, *positive*, and *vigorous*.

In the moment of conclusion the preacher should directly confront each individual personally with the truth and challenge of his message. Each person must be made to feel that the message has been addressed to him and no other. While the spirit and attitude of the preacher greatly contribute to the achieving of personal response, his diction and word choice are also important. The use of personal pronouns—especially *you, your, yours, we, us, our, ours*—give the message a direct, warm, personal touch. Without any trace of nagging or anger but with every evidence of sincere concern to help each one personally, the preacher must deliver the conclusion as well as the whole sermon.

The conclusion should also be specific. While generalities are dangerous in any part of a sermon, they are absolutely fatal in the conclusion. The "perhaps-you-need-this-message" approach will not move men to action. Insofar as possible, the use of concrete terms rather than abstract words or ideas will enable the hearers to grasp meaning, which they must do before they can respond.

The positive conclusion will appeal to more hearts than the

negative conclusion. People usually respond better to affirmative pleas and exhortations than to threats and warnings. Occasionally, a preacher will apply "shock treatment" to his audience by using threats in his conclusion. If this method were ever effective and valid, it is seldom useful today.

The conclusion should be forceful and vigorous. This is not to say that the preacher should speak in loud or shrill tones or that he should stagger to and through the conclusion with his coat off, his sleeves rolled up, his collar unbuttoned, his tie off, and his voice a hoarse whisper. These antics constitute neither force nor "spiritual preaching." Force or emphasis must be an integral part of the content of the conclusion, which must be delivered energetically with a sense of urgency. The congregation must feel that the message makes a difference, a very real difference.

Types of Conclusions

Application type.—Personal application is one basic type of sermon ending. In concluding messages which have dealt with considerable historical material without continuous application, the preacher needs to relate the meaning of the message to those present. Even in sermons in which application is an integral part of the main parts, or in sermons in which application is interwoven into the discussion, one invariably finds it necessary to make pointed and personal application in the conclusion. No attempt should be made to dominate the will of a person, but gentle and earnest application should be laid on the person's heart.

Illustration type.—A second form of conclusion is the illustration, which has become a popular form in the mid-twentieth century. Great skill is required in selecting and preparing an illustration which will throw light upon the specific objective and at the same time will not pervert the feelings and emotions of the people. An illustration, of course, should move people, but it should do so without improper pressure. This type of conclusion is most effective when it illuminates the desired goal

and when it motivates all to want to attain the goal before
them. With proper preparation and adequate restraint the illustration type conclusion is most effective.

Direct appeal.—In the message which presents a challenge to
overt action, the direct appeal or exhortation type of conclusion
is recommended. The character of the direct appeal is shaped
by the proposition and the specific objective. In each instance
the appeal ought to be *to do* what the specific objective sets out.
The pastor in his message can present a need for salvation and
a method of response. In the conclusion a most effective approach is to plead for action on the basis of the message. In an
evangelistic type sermon the action called for is that lost men
repent and turn to Jesus. Of course, this form is not limited to
evangelistic preaching. Appeals can be made for Christians to
unite with the church or for young people to respond to God's
call for individuals to be set apart in his service. The appeal or
exhortation should be done within the bounds of respect for the
individual's freedom and the work of the Holy Spirit.

Poetic type.—Beautiful religious poetry can be appealing and
moving when it is pertinent in content and interpreted with
feeling. Although some men have turned from this approach
because of the common cliché about preaching—"three points
and a poem"—a preacher with a genuine love for poetry need
not abandon this device. He should, perhaps, restrict his use of
poetry and take proper precaution that his poetry is of a high
quality.

Summary type.—The summary type conclusion may be used
in several ways. First, the summary may be a reiteration or a
re-emphasis of the *text*. Second, the summary may stress the
title again by way of definition, elaboration, or application.
Third, the most frequent use of the summary is the recapitula-
tion of the major *body* points. While this is usually a rather
mechanical procedure, it need not be so. The pastor can restate
his points with vigor and freshness and can avoid the dull approach which seems to say, "Well, I must finish some way, so
please listen to my points again." A fourth form for the sum-

mary type is a renewed emphasis of the *thesis* and *specific objective*.

The various types of conclusions may be used singly or in combination. In one sermon the preacher might devote a paragraph to each of the five types, or he might limit the conclusion to one or two major types. The form of the conclusion should vary from sermon to sermon.

Regardless of the type conclusion used, the transition from the body to the conclusion should move smoothly and easily. No pet word or phrase should be a clue that the conclusion is near. The congregation should be pleasantly surprised that the end has arrived.

The Introduction

The introduction is that part of the sermon designed for the presentation of the sermon idea and its relation to the text and the audience. These goals may be accomplished by reading the text and/or by stating the thesis, specific objective, and title of the sermon. In every instance the preacher should be careful to see that the basic purposes of the introduction are clearly accomplished. The introduction presents the issue of the sermon with the clear intention that the body will develop this issue.

The introduction should not be written until the rough draft of the body and the conclusion has been finished. At this stage of composition the introduction is more easily phrased and is likely to be more complete, more appropriate, and more inclusive than at any other step in sermon-building. It is at this point that the first crisis in the preaching situation is encountered. From the moment the first sentence begins, through the next three or four minutes, the battle for attention may be won or lost. Though a successful introduction does not guarantee the success of the total message, a good beginning is invaluable.

Roughly 10 to 15 per cent of the sermon content may be devoted to preparing the way for the sermon body. Some introductions may require more time, others less. Insofar as possible they should be briefly stated.

In order to keep the introduction brief and to the point, annoying distractions should be omitted. One distraction is the injection of apology into the introduction. Except in the rarest circumstance, the preacher need not apologize for his appearance, health, preparation, subject, or anything else. If it is obvious that he is ill, the congregation will be sympathetic. If he is unprepared, the audience will know it soon enough without his telling them. If a subject has been assigned and accepted, it should be treated without apology.

Using humor in the introduction just for the sake of humor consumes unnecessary time and contributes little or nothing to the success of the sermon. This is not to say that humor has no legitimate place in preaching. It can be most effective when it is appropriately used. The recitation of one funny but unrelated story after another, however, may give the congregation the impression it is observing a court jester of a king rather than a prophet of the Most High.

Equally annoying to a congregation is the inclusion of elaborate greetings in the introduction. There are, of course, times when it is appropriate to bring greetings. But those extended expressions heard from many pulpits are rarely justifiable.

In contrast to the elements which tend to distract is the use of prayer immediately preceding the introduction. The preacher may simply say as he steps to the sacred desk, "Will you join me in prayer?" As he leads the waiting congregation to the throne of grace, he creates immediately a spiritual atmosphere conducive to effective preaching and its reception in the hearts and minds of the people.

Purposes of the Introduction

The primary purposes of the introduction are to arouse the interest of the hearers, to make clear the purpose of the sermon, and to create empathy between preacher and congregation.

Every alert preacher knows that he must start where his people are. If he starts where they are, he has a possibility of taking them where he wants them to go. The introduction is supremely important because it makes the initial and probably lasting impression on the people, and it is the time and place for securing interest, understanding, and empathy. If these three are missed early in the message, the sermon will fail. If they are secured, the sermon can succeed. Thus, the introduction is critically important to the success of the sermon.

The initial sentence of the introduction must be so phrased as to attract immediate attention. The people must feel from the very beginning that the message is of vital concern to them and that they want to listen further. Any one of many literary devices will help get the sermon off to a good start: an unusual illustration, a vivid word picture, a challenging question, a bit of conversation, a line of poetry, a pertinent anecdote, or a startling statement, statistic, or fact.

Within the introduction should be a statement of the central idea of the sermon, the introduction of the text, and the presentation of the title. The presentation of these items helps the congregation to understand the direction in which the sermon will move. In clarifying his ideas, the preacher may give facts which explain the choice of title, or he may give information necessary to the understanding of the title. He will, of course, do this in the most interesting way he can.

The introduction is also important in establishing a friendly tone or feeling. It reveals the preacher's attitude toward his people and toward himself. A pastor who speaks to his people as if he is the only one present who has not "bowed the knee to Baal" will incur hostility from his people. Even if a message of rebuke is to be given, it is best not to begin the rebuke in the introduction. The preacher defeats his purpose if he antagonizes his listeners as soon as he begins. If he will remember that he is largely speaking to friends, he will create a feeling of empathy in his introduction.

Types of Introductions

The following are suggested ways in which the introduction may be developed. On some occasions one type will be suffi-

STEPS TO THE SERMON

cient, but usually a combination of several will be required to furnish an adequate setting for the sermon.

The textual introduction.—There are numerous variations of the textual introduction—an old but valuable method of introduction—and this type should be used in some form in each message. It includes introducing and reading the text to the assembled congregation. At least this much of the textual type should be employed in each sermon. Variations of the textual form are (1) an explanation of the pertinent factors (historical, grammatical, rhetorical, practical, comparative, lexical, and spiritual) related to this passage of Scripture and (2) an explanation of the immediate text in relation to its context or to the book of the Bible in which the text is found.

The title or topical approach.—Another kind of introduction which should be used in every sermon is the topical type. It includes at least the announcing of the topic and may sometimes include the definition, explanation, or illustration of one or more words in the title.

The thesis and specific objective approach.—The pastor may utilize either the thesis or the specific objective or both in the introduction. Since, ideally, they are both rather concisely stated, a discussion or explanation of either or both may be included. The textual, topical, thesis, and specific objective types of introduction should be used, at least in part, in each sermon. They may be combined with the types which follow to provide variety and interest.

The life situation type.—The life situation type is the same approach as the "problem beginning" and "the psychological type." The introduction deals with a problem confronting the congregation, and the sermon body usually presents a biblical solution to the problem. Few introductions can be more trite and useless or more profound and helpful than those of this type.

The striking quotation introduction.—The oft-quoted sentence from President Franklin D. Roosevelt, "the only thing to fear is fear," is a good example of the striking quotation introduction. Quotations from Scripture, from the newspaper, from literature, or from some personal experience may be chosen so long as they are pertinent and arrest attention immediately. Because the quotation type is usually brief, it must be used in conjunction with other forms of introductions.

The illustration introduction.—One of the favorite types of introductions is the illustration. The varieties of illustrations available make this form an extremely flexible one. When the illustration is pertinent, well told, and fresh, it makes a valuable contribution to the introduction.

The special occasion approach.—On special occasions carefully prepared remarks about the occasion can be used effectively. Always the preacher who waits until he is on his feet to prepare appropriate words about a special event or occasion will find that he flounders or fails. If he has prepared the sermon with the occasion in view, however, some well-planned reference to the occasion in the introduction is fitting and effective.

The question type approach.—A searching and interesting question which is relevant and answerable is a most appealing way to introduce a message. The question, having been raised in the introduction, is treated in the sermon body.

The object lesson introduction.—Occasionally one may use material objects—a coin, an old book, or some other item of interest—as part of an introduction. Provided that the theme and object are in good taste, the object lesson introduction usually catches interest quickly. "Look" is a fascinating word to children of all ages. When the preacher says, "Look, I want to show you the type of sword used by Simon Peter when he cut off the servant's ear," he will have immediate attention. This method can easily become ludicrous and should be used with caution and good taste.

The Invitation

The invitation is the portion of the sermon in which the pastor issues a challenge to the congregation. It is that part of the service in which the preacher, on the basis of the sermon, tells the audience in specific terms what he believes God wants them to do. It offers individuals an opportunity to act on the truth of the sermon preached. Beginning immediately after the last sentence of the conclusion, the invitation is both a part of the sermon and a part of the worship service.

So important is the decision time that the preacher should carefully train his fellow Christians to respect the invitational period. It is extremely distressing to see Christian people "bolt for the exit" the minute the invitation is announced. Many prominent evangelists boldly say, "If you must leave early, leave while I am preaching. Please do not leave while I am inviting people to come to the Lord." The reason for this is quite obvious. Movements, noises, and distractions cause persons under conviction to turn their minds from their decisions toward the activity about them. The pastor is obligated to instruct his people so that they will stay throughout the invitation, to take part in the invitation by singing, by praying, or by doing whatever is appropriate for the moment.

Like every other part of the sermon, the invitation should be carefully planned and written out. Unless the preacher knows specifically the response he desires from the people, they are likely not to know what they are expected to do. The minister should know before he finishes his message exactly what invitations he will present to the congregation.

An indication as to the type of invitation to be extended may be given early in the service. It is possible for the pastor to indicate at the very beginning of the service that the purpose of the service is evangelistic and that when the sermon closes an invitation will be given to those without Christ. This type of invitation is usually embodied in the introduction and involves a frank and open statement of purpose for the hour. Often the invitation is combined with the conclusion. During the conclusion the preacher may integrate concrete statements of desire. Then all that remains to be done at the invitation period is to give the people an opportunity to respond.

Some preachers at the conclusion of the sermon ask the

people to stand, and then they announce the invitation. This is often an unsatisfactory method because people are putting on coats, reaching for hymnbooks, caring for children, and making plans for getting out of the building while the invitation is being explained.

The most favorable time for extending the invitation is at the end of the conclusion. While the people are still seated, while they are still listening, and before they have had time to realize that a transition has been made, the preacher can state quietly, firmly, and precisely what it is he wishes them to do. After definite directions have been given, he can request the audience to stand, to sing, and to respond. This method takes advantage of the best use of focused attention and is probably the most effective method of giving an invitation.

The preacher must plan his entire worship service carefully in order to provide adequate time for an unhurried invitation. This may mean a shorter sermon, fewer announcements, one less hymn, or any number of things. It is imperative that sufficient time be saved for the invitation.

Not only must he allow sufficient time for the invitation, the preacher must also plan to conclude the invitation when it is evident that God has stopped working. A common complaint among laymen today is that the preacher presumes on the right of God when he continues to prolong an invitation beyond the obvious moment nothing is going to happen. Although a congregation of dedicated Christians will be alert and interested in the invitation as long as they are convinced something dramatic, dynamic, and spiritual is happening, they have every right to expect that the preacher will stop his invitation as soon as it is obvious that the response has ended.

Scope of Invitation

The primary invitation should be prepared in harmony with the specific objective of the sermon. If the specific objective is to get lost men to trust Christ as Saviour, the invitation will be directed toward lost men. If the specific objective is to get

Christians to be good stewards of their material resources, the invitation should be to challenge people to tithe and to give of their material resources to the Lord.

Since the pastor will almost always preach to an audience composed of people with many different needs, he must make adequate preparation for invitations in addition to the one which develops the specific objective. While it is a cardinal principle of sermon preparation that the sermon be directed to one specific group, it is also a basic principle that preparation should be made to reach other groups present. When the pastor comes to his invitation, he should first appeal to the group to whom he has preached. At the same time he will analyze his audience in advance, as best he can, and write out, if needed, a second, a third, and a fourth invitation. For example, if the message has been on Christian stewardship, the first invitation will be for Christians to be good stewards. Then the other appeals—to Baptists to join the fellowship of the church, to young people to surrender to the will of God, and to backsliders to return to the fellowship—are given at the proper time.

As a general rule, the presentation of one invitation at a time is desirable. The pastor will state to the congregation the nature of his primary invitation. Then, he will allow his people to stand and to sing while they are given opportunity for action on the basis of his appeal. After a proper amount of time has passed, the pastor can state his second invitation, call for continued singing, and provide further opportunity for action. This procedure allows time for concentration upon each invitation. There are times, however, because of the size of the audience, a pressing time schedule, the nature of the audience, or other factors within the congregation known only to the pastor, when it is permissible and advisable to announce all of the invitations at one time. If this plan is followed, the pastor will state to his congregation that he has three invitations or three appeals for this service. He will list them one, two, three in specific and definite terms, and call for singing and for action on the part of those needing to make changes in their lives.

Types of Response

An additional element the preacher must consider in preparing the invitation pertains to the kind of response he seeks from his people. He may call for an overt action or a "walking the aisle" type of response. Or he may appeal for the type of decision known only to the individual and God. Many specific invitations call for no open or public decisions, but they do call for decisions within the heart. If the sermon has been of such nature that no overt action is sought, the pastor may have a prayer of dedication at the end of the invitation in which he asks the Lord to help the people practice the truth of the message. Again, the pastor may ask the people to confer with him privately if they need additional guidance in implementing their decisions.

Reliance upon the Lord

The absolutely indispensable element in giving an invitation is reliance upon the Lord. The preacher must never use a single trick that will get one individual to make a false step. High pressure must never be used in an invitation. The preacher is obligated to use cautiously the "professional" devices of hand raising, of having the congregation to stand, of having some to be seated while others remain standing, or of having some close their eyes while others look. Such devices easily degenerate to psychological tricks. At all times the preacher must remember that unless the Spirit of God moves an individual to make a public decision, great damage can be done by some device which causes that person to take a stand which he does not mean. An individual can be brought into the church without a genuine Christian experience, and his last state will be worse than his first. Because a person leaves his place and walks down the aisle does not guarantee that his life has been changed or that anything spiritual has happened to him. It may mean simply that his emotions have been stirred, that his mind has been temporarily captured, and that he is responding to the warmth or the dramatics of the man standing before the church.

It is supremely important that the preacher develop a philosophy of trusting the Lord in the matter of giving invitations. Undoubtedly this appears to be a slow method, but it is much better to go slowly and have positive, eternal results than to move in a manner unseemly to the Lord and to spiritually minded people. One must trust the Lord in giving an invitation and the results will be satisfactory.

Classifying the Sermon

When the preacher has completed the first draft of his sermon, he should analyze and classify it by one or more systems of classification. Throughout this textbook, utility has taken precedence over theory. It does so now in this moment of classification. That a preacher shall produce a message which is useful to his people is of more importance than that he shall produce a particular type sermon. Even though this is true, the task of sermon-building has not been completed until the product is classified.

How does one classify a sermon? Many efforts have been made in the past, but no one system has been completely satisfactory. Perhaps one reason for this lack of satisfaction has been that the various methods of classification have been too restricted. If a certain classification fitted one set of details, it ignored or overlooked another set of details. It is now thought that several systems of classification may be applied to a given sermon.

In general, sermons have been classified in one or more of eight ways: the form or source of the sermon points, the length of the text, the arrangement of the sermon points, time, special forms, the occasional sermon, function or purpose, and content. *Of the eight, purpose and content are the most important.*

For centuries sermons have been classified by form or by the source of the sermon points. In this classification the traditional and best-known one, the *topical sermon,* secures its points primarily from the title or topic while the *expository sermon* secures its major and first subpoints primarily from the text.

The *textual sermon*, an unusual blend of these two, secures its major points from the text and its minor points from the title or from any other source.

In some systems of classification the *length* of the Scripture passage has played a significant role. In this method a careful treatment of a long passage of Scripture (three or more verses) is considered a *biblical* sermon, while a careful treatment of a short passage of Scripture (two verses or less) is considered to be a *textual* sermon.

The arrangement of the sermon points in relation to the Scripture material has furnished a method of classifying sermons as *analytical* or *synthetical*. When the order of the points is the same in the sermon and in the text, the sermon is classified as *analytical*. On the other hand, if the preacher rearranges the order of his points so that they are not in a similar position in the text, the sermon is classified as *synthetical*.

The element of time has entered into sermon classification. *Historical* sermons are those in which the points of the sermon treat the material in the past tense—"in the historical"—while *contemporary* sermons are those which "translate" the material into current significance and write the points in the present tense.

Special forms abound in homiletical literature.[36] One can find the book sermon, the chapter sermon, the paragraph sermon, the life situation message, the jewel sermon, the biographical sermon, the ladder sermon, the Roman candle sermon, the classification sermon, the skyrocket sermon, the twin sermon, and the surprise-package sermon.

Sermons are also classified as *occasional sermons*. In this grouping are the funeral message, the revival sermon, the baccalaureate address, the chapel message, and the dedicatory sermon.

The *function* or *purpose* of the message has provided a useful means of identification for sermons. In this grouping one finds the evangelistic sermon, the didactic message, the actional or

---

[36] See Blackwood, *The Preparation of Sermons,* and Luccock, *op. cit.*

consecrative sermon, the ethical or moral message, the supportive or pastoral message, and the devotional or worship sermon. In addition to these standard groupings one also finds the analytical sermon, designed to cause people to probe the depths of their minds, and the repressive inspirational form, designed to cause people to repress negative thoughts and moods and to be inspired, uplifted, and encouraged.

The contemporary emphasis in the area of sermon classification is classification according to *content*. This procedure identifies the *biblical* sermon as the one which develops the essence of a passage of Scripture. The organizing principle of this sermon form is the text. The unity of the form is seen in the thesis, purpose, and title as they capture the "heart" of the text. There are two forms of biblical sermons: the formal or organized biblical message and the informal biblical message, or the homily. The formal biblical sermon is composed of a planned systematic body structure. When the body development of a biblical sermon is presented in the free form of a continuous comment upon the passage of Scripture (verse by verse without a systematic structure of sermon points) it is called a homily.

The second classification according to content is the *topical-biblical* sermon, improperly called the topical sermon. The topical-biblical sermon has a genuine relationship to the text though not as direct as the biblical sermon. It develops the title primarily and the text secondarily or indirectly by induction, deduction, analogy, comparison and contrast, rhetorical suggestion, or some other indirect method.

A third sermon form according to content is a *combination type*, made up of the biblical and the topical-biblical sermon. In this type the preacher may have, in a four-point sermon, two complete points which develop the very essence of the text and two points which develop the text indirectly and the title directly. The possible number of combinations of this type is unlimited.

Finally, there is the moral or spiritual essay sometimes called a sermon. This message may have a text which the preacher may even announce and read, but he does not develop the text in the sermon body. This is not a recommended sermon form.

One sermon may be identified in several or all of the eight forms of classification. For example, a preacher may secure his points directly (expository) from a long passage of Scripture (biblical), arrange these points in the same order in which they occur in the text (analytical), and state each point in the present tense (contemporary). The message may be a chapter sermon (special forms) for a revival meeting (occasional) for the purpose of presenting Christ to lost men (evangelistic). It may be all of these at the same time and also be a sermon which is biblical in content.

How then is the sermon classified? One may not assign it to any one group but recognize that it has a multiple classification. However, a classification which includes identification as to *purpose* and *content* is usually sufficient. In the theoretical sermon mentioned in the preceding paragraph, it would be enough to say that it is a biblical evangelistic sermon. *The ideal sermon will be as biblical in content and as functional in meeting a definite need as possible.*

VII

Finishing the Sermon

The sermon is not completed when its outline is finished. A final and, in many ways, a most important step in preparation is taken when the minister matures the style in which he will preach the sermon. By style is meant the individual form of expression in which a speaker communicates his thoughts. Style is the manner rather than the matter of preaching. In the largest sense, style involves all of the structure of the sermon—the title, introduction, body, conclusion, and invitation. But in the more limited sense it has to do with the clarity, interest, and force of language. The sermon is "finished" only when the preacher has thought of the language in which he will seek to communicate his ideas to the people.

The Importance of Style

The most important consideration for preaching is content. But is it enough simply to have "something to say"? Content is more important than style, but it does not follow that style is unimportant. A study of the literature of preaching reveals that writers in certain periods emphasize style and form to the neglect of content, while in other periods the accent is almost totally reversed. Either extreme is unfortunate. H. Grady Davis is correct when he insists that substance and style go together. He writes, "The character and dimensions of a thought, its weight, its reach and force, are either limited or extended by the form of its expression. A thought does not seem the same when said indifferently as when said well. When the form is right, form and thought become one." [1]

[1] *Design for Preaching* (Philadelphia: Muhlenberg Press, 1958), p. 4.

Style, then, makes content clear and memorable. As a vehicle of communication, it is of vital interest to the minister. Only when style is considered an end in itself or when all sermons are forced into the same style is the emphasis exaggerated. Several facts about preaching make a consideration of style important.

Preaching Is Communication

The aim of preaching is to win a response. The pulpit is not a lecture platform; the sermon is not a lecture. The preacher's purpose is not merely to capture the ear and the mind of his hearers that he may dispense information. More than this, he yearns to capture their wills, that they may respond to the objective of the sermon. To do so, he must engage in a dialogue with the audience. Effective preaching, then, involves the communication of the Word of God.

Preaching Is Communication with a Complex Audience

It is no small task to communicate with an audience. The first problem which the minister encounters is the complex nature of his hearers. They are, when he begins to preach, much more like a crowd than a congregation. They represent such varied backgrounds and interests that they are not quickly united into one listening group. One writer describes a typical audience:

There are the regulars, whom nothing could keep away from church as long as they are vertical. There are the interested new ones, whose attendance, at least in the beginning, will shame even the regulars. There are the curiosity seekers, and the God-fearers who are earnestly searching for something organized religion has not so far given them. There are the penitents, and the alcoholics, and the new families in town, and the social climbers, and the frustrated musicians, and the man who heard you tell a funny story at the Rotary Club and hopes your sermons are like that, and the parents of children in the nursery, and the voluntary choir, and the man running for Congress.[2]

[2] Stephen F. Bayne, Jr., *Enter with Joy* (Greenwich, Conn.: The Seabury Press, 1961), p. 83.

This picture is not overdrawn; church congregations usually are this complex. They are complex by reason of motivation. Webb Garrison lists ten motivations for church attendance: loyalty to an institution, habit, fellowship, worship, desire for information, respect for traditional authority, curiosity, exhibition, emotional outlet, and a search for the solution of some personal problem.[3] Such varied motivation inevitably results in difficulty of communication.

The complexity of the preaching situation is also found in the varying needs of the people. If he really *sees* his people, the minister may see before him on just any Sunday morning the non-Christian to whom he has spoken in the last week; the alcoholic whom he has rescued from some crisis in the wee small hours; the young college girl who in his study a few days before wept out her confession of immorality; a couple whose marriage is heading for divorce; a woman who is tormented by a guilt complex that has her on the fringe of insanity; parents who have just lost a child; a businessman fighting with temptation; a professional man alienated from a colleague and fellow church member; the aged and the lonely; the disturbed and the frustrated. Each of these in his own spiritual need looks to the minister for a word from God.

Audiences are also complex because of differences in age and spiritual discernment. People differ in interests and in intellectual ability and attainment. They vary as to culture and the social graces. They occupy various positions in business, the professions, and labor.

Besides the complex nature of the congregation there are also psychological barriers to listening. It is true that the minister wins a certain authority by nature of his role as a servant of God. If the man speaking is a beloved and respected pastor, the people will want to hear him. But there are also hindrances to attention in the preaching situation. This same man spoke to the same people about the same general subject last Sunday and the Sunday before. Unless he is alert and makes his sermon vibrant

---

[3] Garrison, *op. cit.*, pp. 27-35.

with arresting and vivid energy and style, his congregation, in spite of its respect for him, will tend to "tune him out."

The problem is deepened by the sheer impossibility of sustained attention. The hearer desires to listen attentively, but his ability to listen without deviation is limited to a few seconds or minutes. When the distractions of architecture, building temperature, outside and inside noises, and the other interests of the hearer are added, sustained attention becomes a serious problem.

It is the responsibility of the minister to mold such a *crowd*, under such circumstances, into a listening *congregation*. Perhaps he will never achieve absolute success in this polarity of attention. But try he must. His success in this area depends largely upon his style. He must use language which will gain and regain attention and which will be clear and relevant to all his hearers.

Preaching Is Oral Communication

Style is important also because preaching is oral communication. The ministerial student often is dismayed to discover that the written sermon which receives an excellent grade in homiletics class may not win similar acclaim when preached. The problem may simply be that the student and teacher have neglected to note the differences between written and oral style. Although they share many qualities, there is enough difference between them that what is excellent in one may be inferior in the other. Language is of vital significance to the minister because he must always translate his ideas into *oral* style.

Several important differences between oral and written style should be considered. Perhaps the major one is that in oral communication impressions and meanings must be made clear in a moment. The hearer has no opportunity to study the sermon for definition of terms or for impressions missed in the first moment of delivery. Oral communication occurs immediately, or it does not occur at all. For this reason it is correct to refer to the sermon as a "movement in time." [4] Each moment of the ser-

---

[4] Davis, *op. cit.*, p. 163.

mon must be clear, and each must fit into the total pattern so that ultimately the hearers grasp the sermon as one unit of thought. The only means of communication in preaching are words and gestures. The moods and meanings of the sermon must be evident in the minister's words, voice, and body.

Oral style is more personal than written style. The speaker is not limited to the formal style of a literary manuscript. While his grammar should be correct, he should use more personal and conversational language than is usually found in formal written style. Personal illustrations are appropriate and powerful. The informality of oral style strengthens the hearer's ability to "listen" to the sermon.

The speaker's ability to communicate complex ideas is usually limited in preaching. His appeal must be direct and straightforward. Figures of speech, simple words and sentences, language which appeals to the eye as well as to the ear—these are characteristic of direct oral style. Such necessities of oral communication impose a responsibility upon the minister to mature his style.

Preaching Is Communication with *This* Generation

No consideration should demonstrate the importance of style more vividly than the fact that the minister must speak to people who live today. He must speak to this generation, to people of this *culture*. He must be relevant.

In 1928 Harry Emerson Fosdick startled the homiletic world by stating that the trouble with much preaching is that it is not interesting. "It takes for granted in the minds of the people ways of thinking which are not there, misses the vital concerns which are there, and in consequence uses a method of approach which does not function." [5] Fosdick's point is that the minister must preach to the contemporary hearer. He must speak to the people as they are—their problems, their needs, their culture. Here is a truth about preaching which cannot be denied.

---

[5] "What Is the Matter with Preaching?" *Harper's Magazine*, CLVII (July, 1928), 134.

The problems of speaking to the contemporary hearer have stimulated an intensive study in Christian communication. The questions raised in this study involve the nature of the contemporary hearer, biblical interpretation, and whether it is possible to speak to today's culture in the traditional "symbols" of the gospel. One such study will demonstrate the seriousness of the problem.

James E. Sellers, in a stimulating work in communication, insists that there is a sense in which every hearer is an "outsider" to the Word of God. To him the problem of communication is that the minister faces a "post-Christian" society in which everyone is an "outsider," in one of two varieties.[6] He is either a non-Christian who "accidentally" embraces certain Christian concepts and values, or he is a nominal Christian who professes faith but who pursues the ordinary goals and secular purposes of the age. In either case communication with the contemporary hearer is difficult: the non-Christian feels he is a Christian because he lives by "Christian principles," and the Christian acts like the non-Christian while living in the security of his church. How can the minister be relevant in such a culture? How can he actually find a point of contact in which the hearer will see his need of the gospel? Sellers finds the answer partially in communication in language "that outsiders can understand." [7] Traditional Christian symbols, he argues, may have to give way to newer symbols which touch the "outsider" at some point of conflict and through which the gospel may be made meaningful to him. Such is one effort to deal with the problem of speaking to men who live *today*. Bultmann's demythologizing and Tillich's communication by "existential significance" are efforts in the same direction.

Of course, those efforts at relevance which by their hermeneutical method seem to question the importance of the historical are of doubtful value. The biblical expositor can have the

---

[6] James E. Sellers, *The Outsider and the Word of God* (Nashville: Abingdon Press, 1961), p. 21.

[7] *Ibid.*, p. 23.

faith to believe, with James Stewart, that when he preaches the message of the Scriptures, "God is coming forth to encounter us with incomparable blessings in his hand" and that in this message one is "confronted . . . with the living Christ." [8] Still the need persists for a preaching style which makes the gospel applicable to man as he is today. Relevance is not a matter of poor hermeneutics or theology. It is properly a matter of style.

The minister must speak the language of today. He must speak to the point of need in today's world. He cannot ignore the thinking and culture of today's audience. The minister who wins the ear of today's listener is the minister who works continually on the relevance of his style.

Elements of Effective Style

Clarity

The sermon originally is an idea in the mind of the preacher. This idea is then offered to others in the symbols of language. Unless these symbols mean the same thing to the preacher and his hearers, communication does not occur. Effective style, therefore, is first of all a matter of clarity. The minister must be understood. No higher tribute can be paid to the preacher than that offered to John Wesley: "He began with an elaborate style, but as his intelligent servant Betty could not understand him he changed it. His aim was to address the bulk of mankind. . . . He labored to avoid all words which were not easily understood or not used in common conversation." [9] The style of those who speak to the masses is clear.

It should be obvious that clarity involves a great deal more than the use of short, simple words. Clarity begins in the mind of the minister and involves his identity with people as well as the structure of his language. The routes to clarity are many.

Clarity through the sermon thesis and objective.—If the minister is to have a clear style he must think clearly about the

[8] "Exposition and Encounter," *Encounter,* XIX (Spring, 1958), 169.
[9] Oscar Sherwin, *John Wesley, Friend of the People* (New York: Twayne Publishers, Inc., 1961), pp. 86-87.

sermon he is to deliver. If he does not understand what he wishes to say, it is certain that his hearers will not understand. W. Somerset Maugham observes: "Another cause of obscurity is that the writer is himself not quite sure of his meaning. He has a vague impression of what he wants to say, but has not, either from lack of mental power or from laziness, exactly formulated it in his mind." [10] What is said about the writer can be said about the preacher. The sermon must be clear to him if it is to be clear to others.

If the minister is thinking clearly about his sermon, he is able to reduce its message to a simple sentence. This sentence has been called the sermon proposition. [11] If the sermon is not capable of such reduction, it is likely too complex for clear understanding by an audience. Concerning the importance of the proposition for clarity, John Henry Jowett writes,

Do not confuse obscurity with profundity, and do not imagine that lucidity is necessarily shallow. Let the preacher bind himself to the pursuit of clear conceptions, and let him aid his pursuit by demanding that every sermon he preaches shall express its theme and purpose in a sentence as lucid as his powers can command. [12]

The minister should also understand his sermon objective if he expects to be clear. Many sermons lack clarity because they do not seem to move toward any definite objective. Preaching must have more purpose than to satisfy a Sunday morning custom. Every sermon should have a specific objective—a response sought, a purpose to be realized. If the minister has such a goal and moves toward it as directly as possible, he will enhance the clarity of his sermon.

Clarity through a knowledge of the hearers.—Clarity is also a matter of identification with the audience. If the speaker fails to understand his audience his potential for clarity is greatly

---

[10] *The Summing Up* (New York: Doubleday, Doran & Co., 1938), p. 31.

[11] See pp. 43-44.

[12] *Op. cit.*, pp. 133-34.

reduced. This is true because the meaning of words is always determined by usage rather than by dictionary definition. Audiences understand the minister according to their cultural and intellectual backgrounds. Clarity demands that the preacher "acquaint himself with the point at which his hearers are, and begin from there, and not from uninformed assumptions about their situation." [13]

The minister should neither "speak down" to his hearers nor talk "over their heads." He should speak at the level of conversational language which will be grasped by the majority of his audience. This rule of clarity demands that the speaker both understand and identify himself with his hearers. He must have such a compassion for them that his greatest desire is to speak to their needs. Such an identification will mean that the style in which a sermon is delivered will vary with the occasion. The wise preacher does not use the same style in the university chapel as in the downtown mission. Jesus spoke clearly to people because he adjusted his language to the situation. When the setting was pastoral, he spoke in the language of the shepherd. He just as easily spoke to fishermen, farmers, and merchants in their language. Such a compassionate identity with the people can inspire the modern minister to be clear. If he desires above all else to help men find God, no effort at clarity will be too costly.

Clarity through language.—A discussion of clarity usually deals with proper word choice and sentence structure because the greatest single barrier to understanding is the problem of language. As mentioned above, the meaning of words does not exist apart from culture. Definitions are determined by usage. Words mean different things to different people at different times. Thus, "each time a word is used in a sentence both the context of the word and the background of the reader or hearer limit and direct its exact meaning." [14] The problem is especially

---

[13] Donald O. Soper, *The Advocacy of the Gospel* (New York: Abingdon Press, 1961), p. 35.
[14] Garrison, *op. cit.*, p. 60.

acute in the case of abstract terms. What does "truth" mean?
What does the word "father" mean? The meaning of such
terms will depend on the individual experience associated with
them. If clarity depends on the use of language symbols which
mean the same thing to the speaker and his hearers, the necessity
of proper word choice and construction becomes evident.
Several facts about clear language should be noted.

1. Choose language that is understandable.—It is much more
important that a word be understood than that it be short. Rudolf Flesch has devised a significant and convenient measurement by which written material may be examined for read-
ability.[15] He grades style from very easy to very difficult,
according to sentence and word length. By the same measurement he estimates the school grade and the percentage of
American adults who find a certain style readable. While this
measurement is important for clarity, it should not be taken to
mean (as, indeed, Flesch does not) that short words alone render
style clear. If words are understandable, the hearer will not
likely take note whether they are short or long.

The minister should avoid technical words in his preaching.
It would be as unwise for him to use technical theological terminology in a sermon as for a physician to describe a patient's
illness to him in medical jargon. Traditional theological terms,
such as "justification," "sanctification," and even such a common term as "faith" may need "translation" into more understandable language. Again, the preacher should not clutter his
sermon with many foreign terms. He particularly should guard
against a pulpit display of his use of the original biblical languages. Many sermons have lost clarity because of the preacher's
constant reference to what "the Greek says" or to what "the
Hebrew form is." The minister should do technical exegesis in
the study and express the fruit of that work in language the
hearers understand.

Language must be in touch with reality; the minister must
use language from life. Soper's criticism of preaching is that

---

[15] *The Art of Readable Writing* (New York: Harper & Bros., 1949), p. 149.

"much of the language in which the Christian Gospel is at present advanced is language which, by linguistic tests, is imprecise, irrelevant, and insignificant." [16] There is no contemporary language source which the minister should neglect. Let him read fiction, the classics, news magazines, newspapers, drama, the dictionary. Let him study the arts, radio, and television. Let him use every help at his disposal to enlarge his vocabulary and to understand the mind of the hearer in order to communicate the eternal message in relevant and understandable terminology.

2. Have a preference for short words.—While short words do not guarantee clarity, they do contribute to lucid style. Davis says, "A man should cultivate a taste, a preference for the short, familiar words when a longer or more exact word is not definitely needed." [17] The minister does not wisely ignore the fact that many of the most memorable addresses and excerpts from literature have been written in brief, simple words. His style will be clear if he prefers the same language for his sermon.

3. Eliminate useless words.—Much preaching style suffers from verbosity. It is cluttered with adjectives, articles, and such empty, useless words as "today," "this morning," or "brethren." One of the primary qualities of clear style is that it says a great deal in a few words. Clear style contains no unnecessary words and no unnecessary sentences. Every word counts. If preaching were freed from many pulpit clichés and empty expressions, it would be both more clear and more vigorous.

4. Choose specific, concrete words.—Clarity demands that words be concrete rather than abstract, specific rather than general. By concrete words is meant words that designate particular things or action. Jesus did not say, "See the world of nature, how it develops." He said, "See the lilies, how they grow," and the impression of God's perfect care is forever clear. A recently published sermon began: "The minister of the church Sir Walter Scott attended was said to have become very frightened when the famous author was present. When Scott

---

[16] *Op. cit.,* p. 36.
[17] *Op. cit.,* p. 271.

heard of it he commented: 'He isn't afraid of God, why is he afraid of me?' " [18] How much clearer this introduction to a sermon on criticism is than if the minister had begun with the general sentence, "Preachers should not be frightened by their audiences." Concrete words and sentences stab the hearer awake. They appeal to his senses. They make the preacher's intention clear and striking.

5. Use well-constructed sentences.—Much that has been said about words can be said about sentences. It is incorrect to think that the only clear sentences are short ones or that every sentence in a sermon should be short. The short sentence serves a purpose. It usually brings an idea into sharp focus. On the other hand, the long sentence summarizes, gathers material together, and makes it "flow." Davis observes that hearers do not listen to effective speech in sentences at all.[19] It is likely that it is only when sentences are monotonously short or long that they interfere with communication. Although he might favor the more frequent use of short sentences, the minister should use a mixture of short and long sentences, making certain that each type is used for its intended purpose.

It is vitally important to clarity that sentences be well constructed. The minister should give attention to the elementary principles of composition.[20] Such a study will reduce the number of complex, awkward sentences, help locate the major idea in the sentence in its proper place, and lead to the use of strong, active verbs.

6. Use conversational language.—The American preacher has often wondered whether he should preach in correct formal English or in correct standard English. A desire for clarity dictates a choice of the latter.

---

[18] Luther Joe Thompson, *Monday Morning Religion* (Nashville: Broadman Press, 1961), p. 53.

[19] *Op. cit.*, p. 276.

[20] A brief but excellent book for this purpose is William Strunk, Jr., *The Elements of Style* (2nd ed.; New York: The Macmillan Co., 1959); see also Davis, *op. cit.*, pp. 274-93; Broadus, *On the Preparation and Delivery of Sermons*, pp. 245-48; Blackwood, *The Preparation of Sermons*, pp. 166-87; and Jones, *op. cit.*, pp. 177-78.

Conversational style involves the use of personal words and sentences. Personal words are personal names, personal pronouns, words of definite masculine and feminine gender, and words of definite personal description, such as "men" or "children." Personal sentences are questions, commands, sentence fragments, exclamations, sentences addressed directly to the audience, and also direct or indirect quotations.[21] Other marks of conversational language are the use of contractions and repetition. In fact, any element of correct conversation may be used in the sermon. Impressed with this need, Garrison believes the preacher who has something to say "does not hesitate to use the same word twice in a sentence, to inject his own personality into the message, to split an occasional infinitive, or even to chop his thoughts into clauses that are not true sentences."[22]

Let the student observe a warning! In spite of the evident value of conversational language, he should not permit his spoken utterance to degenerate into vulgar, sub-standard English. Splitting an infinitive does not guarantee clarity of speech. This rather relaxed approach to language means that the clearest style for preaching is the less formal and more personal language of conversation. The preacher should study the language of the literature and speech which captures the attention of the contemporary hearer and adapt it to sermon use. If this seems to advise the use of fragments or an occasional dangling preposition, the preacher will not remain aloof. He is more interested in reaching people than in passing tests on composition.

Clarity through illustrations.—Clarity is also achieved by the use of frequent illustrations. A good rule to follow is: state and illustrate. This does not mean that every thought of the sermon should be illustrated with a story. It does mean that the minister should make his ideas clear by the use of some form of pictorial language. Such illustration may be accomplished in any one of a dozen ways.

A favorite form of illustration is the figure of speech. The

---

[21] Flesch, *op. cit.*, p. 79.

[22] *Op. cit.*, p. 98.

most frequently used figures are: alliteration, onomatopoeia, metaphor, simile, allegory, hyperbole, and irony. Other forms of illustration which aid clarity include description, narration, the parable, example, quotation, and current events. These cast light on an idea. They help to make it clear.

The following introduction demonstrates the value of illustrative language in the struggle to be clear:

> The college woman came with her thoughtful comment: "So many voices! Which shall I follow?" She confronted the babel of our times. Some cynic has said that man gained the power to speak around the world just at the moment when he has nothing important to say. Sound-truck voices, radio voices, platform voices, television voices, pulpit voices, and voices of our endless arguments bedevil our day. Some voices are greedy: the advertising voices sometimes mean "I want your money"; and the political voices, "I want your vote"; and they have scant regard for the persons to whom they speak. Some voices are frantic, especially when discussing Sputnik. Some proclaim too confidently that they know the way. Some touch only the surface of our need. "So many voices! Which shall I follow?" Perhaps a Voice which is never heard, except silently in silence, yet always heard.[23]

This introduction contains a brief story, an indirect quotation in the form of a striking sentence, excerpts from contemporary experience, descriptive terms, alliteration, and conversational style. The preacher could have said briefly, "Of all the voices which modern man hears, he needs most to hear the voice of God." That was the basic idea, but the rich illustrative material makes the idea both clear and arresting.

Interest

It is not enough to be clear. It is possible to be clear and at the same time to be dull. Effective style reaches the mind by both interest and clarity. The problems of attention which make

---

[23] George A. Buttrick, *Sermons Preached in a University Church* (New York: Abingdon Press, 1959), p. 80.

an interesting style necessary have already been discussed. It is now proper to suggest techniques which help to make style interesting.

Interest through direct approach.—Aside from content, which is of importance to the preacher and also to his hearers, nothing is of more help in arousing interest than the direct approach. This means achieving the immediate involvement of the audience. In the first moment of a skilfully prepared sermon the hearer feels that the minister is speaking directly to him. It is an able preacher, indeed, who can make every hearer ask in the opening moments of every sermon, "How did he know what has been going on in my life this week?"

A direct approach can be made by beginning with the people —raising an issue, stating a problem, asking a question, making a striking statement, offering an illustration which involves them —and then relating the issue to the text. Harry Emerson Fosdick mastered an interesting style. No hearer could ever doubt that Fosdick intended to speak to him. Examples of direct approach in this minister's sermons are legion. In his sermon, "Handling Life's Second Bests," his second sentence is, "We all have to live upon the basis of our second and third choices." [24] After giving a biographical illustration to substantiate this thesis, Fosdick turns to Paul and the text. The sermon is more interesting because it begins with "we all" and not with Paul. This does not mean that Paul occupies any lesser place in the sermon, but the minister can better use Paul after he has involved his hearers. They know that Paul has something to say to them.

Fosdick uses the same technique to incite interest in his sermon, "When Prayer Means Power." The first three sentences are: "There are three ways in which men get what they want— thinking, working, praying. Concerning the first two no one has any doubt. . . . But concerning the third, doubts are plentiful." [25]

George W. Truett was also a master in involving his audience immediately. He began his sermon, "The Highest Welfare of

---

[24] *Riverside Sermons* (New York: Harper & Bros., 1958), p. 54.
[25] *Ibid.*, p. 122.

the Home," with the sentence, "Our text this morning has to do with the highest welfare of those who are bound to us affectionately by ties of flesh and blood and marriage." [26] Notice that he did not say "bound to Lot," although Lot's family is the basis of the sermon, but he says "bound to us." Such direct approach helps the minister gain interest and, if the spirit of involvement continues, to maintain it.

Interest through the present tense.—Closely related to direct approach is the use of the present tense. To preach in the present tense is to make the facts of the sermon clear, to interpret those facts, and to apply them to the hearer.[27] Obviously, present-tense preaching does not mean that the historical content of the sermon is deleted. The biblical sermon rests upon faithful exegesis and presentation of the text. Neither does present-tense preaching refer primarily to the grammar of the sermon. Rather, the text is interpreted and applied to the issues of the contemporary situation.

It is to be admitted that there are certain style helps which are usable in preaching a sermon in the present tense. If titles, opening sentences, and major points are phrased in the present tense, the style is generally more contemporary. "Let the Church Be the Church," for example, obviously awakens interest more than "Paul's Doctrine of Church Discipline." So the structure of this sermon would be best stated in the present tense. But the fact remains that application to the hearer is of primary concern. When the minister does this in dynamic language his sermon becomes vitally important to the hearer. It is in the present tense. It is a *sermon* for today and not a *lecture* on yesterday.

Interest through freshness of approach.—Interest also depends on the creativity of the preacher. One of the first lessons a student should learn in homiletics is that the art of preaching is a fluid art. Few rules of form and style are rigid. After mastering

---

[26] *The Prophet's Mantle* (Nashville: Broadman Press, 1948), p. 29.

[27] Andrew W. Blackwood, *Biographical Preaching for Today* (New York: Abingdon Press, 1954), p. 182.

the key principles of structure, the mature student should dare to be creative. He should experiment with the presentation of old and familiar truths in new settings. He should use fresh sermon forms.[28] Edgar N. Jackson observes that those advertisers who know how to sell their products know the importance of fresh approaches.[29] The minister should also know that nothing makes preaching more dynamic than the genius of new form and expression.

Interest through contrast.—Interest is always heightened by contrast. It is instructive to note how often Jesus used this method in his preaching. Only the Pharisees who were present could adequately tell what a stinging impression he made upon them by the contrast of two sinners in the parable of the prodigal son. If they had eyes to see, they saw themselves in the "respectable sinner" who felt superior to his more openly sinful brother. Contrasting the houses built upon the rock and the sand, Jesus stirred his hearers' interest in his words.

Frederick W. Robertson utilized the principle of interest by contrast in the nineteenth century. His famous two-point sermons often present contrasting ideas and principles. Such style seems to leave an option with the hearer. It calls for the weighing of values and the making of decisions. Such activity makes the hearer an interested participant rather than an indifferent spectator.

The principle of contrast also involves the art of variety of style and delivery within a sermon. Garrison feels that *"the most important single element in commanding attention is contrast, or ordered change."* [30] In the course of a sermon changes of material and style should occur which will make the sermon appeal to the different groups in the audience. Sharp contrasts in style also arrest fleeting attention and return it to the sermon. Such devices as the striking sentence, dramatic narration, the

[28] See pp. 105-18.

[29] *A Psychology for Preaching* (Great Neck, N.Y.: Channel Press, Inc., 1961), p. 24.

[30] Garrison, *op. cit.*, p. 78.

illustration, the demonstration, and wisely chosen humor make contrast possible.

Interest through language.—Aside from the general routes to interest already mentioned, something should be said about the more specific language of interest. All that has been said previously regarding clarity could be repeated in behalf of securing interest. That which makes style clear will usually make it interesting also. At least two devices, however, need new emphasis at this point.

First, personal words and sentences are especially helpful in gaining and holding attention. In his discussion of language, Rudolf Flesch measures human interest by the percentage of personal words and sentences in written material.[31] His conclusion is that the greater the frequency of personal references the more dramatic the style and the higher the "human interest score." Testing his measurement in typical magazines, he found that scientific and trade journals, ordinarily dull to the average reader, use little personal language, but fiction, ordinarily interesting reading, abounds in such language. A justified observation is that sermons which abound in personal words and sentences will be both clear and interesting.

Second, direct, concrete, and active words also make style interesting. Blackwood groups such language under the category "live words," defining such words as "fact words, action words, words with 'hands and feet.' "[32] To be interesting the minister should use concrete nouns and strong, active verbs. These words add life and substance to style. They appeal to the eye as well as to the ear of the listener. They are words that form visual images. They are, as Broadus says of elegance, "the product of imagination."[33] Such words add beauty to the sermon.

Vivid language abounds in the following excerpt from the introduction to Leslie Weatherhead's sermon, "Which Voice Shall I Trust?"

---

[31] *Op. cit.,* p. 151.
[32] *The Preparation of Sermons,* p. 190.
[33] *On the Preparation and Delivery of Sermons,* p. 269.

The dull, monotonous days passed one by one, and then suddenly a child in the Temple dreamed about God. Whatever the explanation of the experience may have been, to Samuel it was a *Voice*, breaking into his uneventful life as a trumpet wakens sleepers at dawn; and it was a voice that changed the course of history.[34]

Such style is interesting because it is alive, it paints pictures, it uses concrete, active words.

Force

Force, another essential in effective style, is usually thought to refer to the energetic delivery which wins a response from the audience. In many respects it is similar to interest. Both win attention, but forceful style does more than win attention. It demonstrates the conviction of the speaker and elicits conviction and decision from the hearer.

Many of the qualities of style which contribute to clarity and interest also make sermons forceful. Broadus lists concrete and specific language, the proper construction of sentences, and figures of speech as requisites to energetic style.[35] Luccock names clarity, contrast and variety in sentences, and concrete language as means of achieving force.[36] It is evident, then, that force is achieved by clarity and interest. To these qualities other elements of style which pertain more uniquely to force should be added.

Force through personality.—Energy of style begins with a forceful personality. In this sense force cannot be mechanically learned. It must be a part of the person's experience and character. To be forceful a speaker must be capable of energetic thought and feeling. Broadus states that this ability of character is the key to true oratory. The preacher may preach acceptable sermons, "but if a man has not force of character, a passionate soul, he will never be really eloquent." [37]

---

[34] *That Immortal Sea* (New York: Abingdon Press, 1953), pp. 35-36.
[35] *On the Preparation and Delivery of Sermons*, pp. 252-68.
[36] *Op. cit.*, pp. 188-90.
[37] *On the Preparation and Delivery of Sermons*, p. 252.

Not only does forceful style reside in a forceful personality, but a minister must also feel deeply about a particular sermon if he is to be energetic. He must deliver his soul on a theme which he believes and knows by experience to be of spiritual worth. In this connection Clovis G. Chappell observes: "If the preacher is to be interesting, he must be interested. . . . If he has lost his sense of the wonder of God's love, if the freshness has gone from his own religious experiences, then he is not likely to be very interested in the gospel that he preaches." [38] Sermons will hold no wonder for others if they hold no wonder for the man who delivers them. Men should preach only that which they believe and desire to bring others to believe. If a man of passionate character preaches such a sermon, the battle for force is half won already.

Force through pronouns.—There is a difference of opinion as to the pronouns which the preacher should use in delivering the sermon. Should he use the first person or the second person pronouns? Should it be "you need to do this" or "we need to do this"? Should the sermon deal with "your problems" or "our problems"?

Since authority and force are closely related, it is likely true that the most forceful preaching is most often done in terms of "you." Certainly prophetic preaching most often demands such style.

But force is also achieved by the minister's identification with his people, never by his separation from them. The minister should never be so spiritually proud as to exclude himself from a need for the gospel. In a sense he always preaches to himself. God has first spoken to him and then through him to the people. The preacher also must worship!

It is correct to say, therefore, that if force is achieved by the use of "you," it is deepened by preaching in the spirit of "we." Though God's spokesman must not hesitate to be boldly direct, he must never become a "man removed from his people." There

---

[38] *Anointed to Preach* (New York: Abingdon-Cokesbury Press, 1951), pp. 52-53.

is force in identity that will heighten the force of courageous proclamation.

Force through virile language.—Forceful style is characterized by strong, virile words. Such words are specific and concrete rather than general and vague. But virile style is more than concrete and personal words. Specifically, forceful language is the language of a man. Luccock describes it as "strong, salty, vascular, and alive." [39] It is a man's "native tongue of earthly speech." Such a description does not imply that forceful language is vulgar or "earthy" in the sense of profanity. Neither does it suggest that forceful style is void of the prose of eloquent quotation and culture. But the minister who is forceful uses language which rings with reality. He is never vague, ethereal, or effeminate. He speaks with the strength of a man who has been with God but who also stands in the arena of life as it is. His language bears the strength and the reality of an Amos or a Jeremiah. He has the power to stab awake the conscience of men. He speaks like a man!

Force through conciseness.—Force is gained by brevity. True brevity, however, is not defined only in terms of time. It is possible for a fifteen-minute sermon to be "long" or for a forty-minute sermon to be "short." True brevity is achieved by conciseness. Concise style is free of useless terminology. The conclusion of the sermon, for example, can lose most of its force if the minister regularly signals the end of the sermon with "and in conclusion," or if he moves from one anticlimax to another without ever seeming to bring the sermon to an end. The forceful preacher moves quickly toward his objective, makes every word meaningful, knows when he arrives at the climax, makes a sharp application and appeal, and is through before the force of his message is lost.

When the techniques of energetic style are combined with positive and meaningful content, the minister is forceful. He speaks for God, and men listen and deal with God for themselves.

---

[39] *Op. cit.*, p. 190.

The Development of Style

A practical question remains. How does the minister develop his style? There is a sense in which every man has a style already, for "style is the man." But if the student of preaching has carefully observed the importance of communication, he will be eager to grow in his style abilities.

Two means of developing effective style have already been mentioned prominently. One is wide reading. The preacher whose sermons are fresh and dynamic is the preacher who is constantly reading. For the sake of style, this reading should include an ever-widening area of material. Certainly the preacher should read in his own field of theology. There is no question that such reading should include the sermons of other men. The fear of plagiarism should not obscure the potential value in studying other preachers and their preaching. Two hints are in order at this point: read the sermons of the master preachers of other generations as well as your own, and study the sermons of the preachers of other denominations than your own. The preacher who does not read and profit from the sermonic work of men who practice the techniques of effective style only impoverishes himself and those to whom he preaches.

The preacher's reading should not be limited to his own field. He cannot afford to neglect any area of literature. Great poetry and the classics can be of high value. The best sellers, both fiction and nonfiction, drama, and other contemporary literature can be of invaluable aid in teaching the art of communication with today's world. It is often true that more style, inspiration, and illustrative material can be gained from one excellent novel than from a dozen books of sermons. The libraries of the great preachers reveal that they have read in the field of fiction, science, philosophy, psychology, and history.

The student of style will be eager to read the notable addresses of statesmen, political leaders, and cultural leaders of his day. He should read regularly at least one news magazine each week and as many periodicals as possible. These will inform him not only on current events but also on the qualities of contemporary style.

Of course, the reading of the Bible is a primary aid to effective communication. For many the Bible is only a quarry of texts; it is largely neglected for devotional and inspirational purposes. But where could one go for better instruction in the use of language than to the beautiful poetry of Psalms, the dynamic utterances of the prophets, or the unsurpassed preaching style of Jesus?

The problem with reading is finding time to do it. When will a busy pastor have the time to read as recommended here? Although it is a difficult problem indeed, the average minister can find more reading time than he imagines. A part of the morning's study program should be set aside for reading that is not associated with sermon preparation. Light reading can be done late in the evening. Much reading can be done while traveling or during engagements which break the routine of the pastoral ministry. Certain seasons of the year offer more reading time than others. Essentially, however, the preacher must discipline himself to read as he disciplines himself in every other area of his work. The route to good style is through good reading habits. At any price, let the minister read, read, read. His profit in the pulpit will justify the investment.

Another means of improving style, mentioned earlier, is a study of the people to whom we preach. It is not too simple to say that to love people and to desire to communicate with them is to grow in the art of self-expression. Effective preaching and effective pastoral care go together. Every contact with the people should give the minister an opportunity to learn their needs, their abilities, their "language." If the people mean more to him than ideas, his ability to communicate will improve with every passing week.

A formal study of communication can also help to develop style. Many colleges and universities have courses in communication. An increasing emphasis on Christian communication and the arts is being made in theological education. Books on effective style and communication are growing more numerous. These sources can be helpful to the minister in the development of his style.

In the final analysis, however, nothing will mature style quite so much as writing. For those who have never written a sermon manuscript, it will seem difficult to believe that there is no moment in the preaching experience except the actual delivery of the sermon which affords so much joy as writing. Often it is possible to write the sermon from beginning to end in one sitting. In such an experience the sermon begins to vibrate with spiritual life. At other times writing requires long hours of labor. In such times the willingness to toil over the style of the sermon carries its own spiritual reward.

Writing the sermon is logically the final step in its maturity. After the idea and objective have been determined, the text exegeted, the material gathered, and the outline formed, it is time to construct the language in which the sermon will be delivered. Every young minister should discipline himself to write his sermons in full. Some teachers suggest that the first ten years of his ministry he should write everything that he plans to say. It is likely just as true that he should continue to write as many sermons as possible throughout his ministry.

The purpose of writing sermons is not necessarily to repeat them in the pulpit just as they have been written. The purpose is to mature oral style. When the minister writes, he actually confronts the manner in which he expresses himself. He "hears" himself as he is. By revision and by continuous practice he develops the qualities of clarity, interest, and force which are essential to effective preaching. If he puts his manuscripts aside completely and goes into the pulpit with or without notes, he will doubtless use much language which he has not written. But the language which he uses there will be just as vital as that chosen for the manuscripts.

A suggested order for finishing a sermon is: (1) with the outline and material in hand, write through the sermon from beginning to end as quickly as possible; (2) correct this rough draft according to the principles of effective style; (3) rewrite, partially or completely, if necessary; (4) put the manuscript aside for several hours and let the mind rest from the sermon; (5) return to the manuscript as the hour for preaching approaches. Read and study the sermon until it becomes a part of you.

Three common objections are brought against the writing program just proposed. One is that writing makes sermons wooden, and this criticism is sometimes justified. It need not be valid, however, if the minister writes for speaking, that is, in oral style, and if he is free from an artificial dependence on the manuscript. Rather, such preparation should give the minister his greatest pulpit liberty.

Some object to writing the sermon because of the time involved. But if the minister follows the steps of preparation outlined in the foregoing chapters, it is already apparent to him that his sermon preparation cannot be confined to the days between one Sunday and the next. It will be planned and executed for weeks in advance of the preaching appointment. The actual writing of the sermon should be done just prior to the time of delivery, but the groundwork should have been accomplished days before. To be sure, such a program is ideal. The busy pastor may not be able to write more than one manuscript each week. But even limited writing will continue to accomplish the purpose of style development. If the ministerial student commits himself to a program of study requiring adequate time for sermon preparation, this habit may well remain with him throughout his life. Thus, he will always *have* time for his primary task—preaching and the preparation to do it.

Others object to writing because they face a psychological difficulty. For some unexplainable reason, they cannot write sermons and deliver them effectively. When this is actually true and is not an excuse for laziness, the minister should discover some other technique by which he may develop style. Some men speak their sermons aloud after an outline has been formulated. Others dictate sermons and later read them for style suggestions.

Some record sermons as they are preached and later criticize them for style defects. Other men who do not write sermons do some other writing and thus develop style. It is fair to say that most ministers who have developed effective style have either written their sermons in full or have found some equally effective substitute for writing.

Let the minister remember that content and style go together. If preaching is a part of God's plan to redeem the world, and if the language of the sermon either limits or extends that purpose in preaching, every discipline which will strengthen the art of communication is worthy.

VIII

Delivering the Sermon

The delivery of the sermon is the most dynamic moment of the preaching experience. In that moment all sermon preparation is brought to fruition or frustration. If the sermon is delivered effectively, the minister, in grateful joy, forgets the long hours of toil in preparation. But if he fails, all his labor in the study haunts him as a heavy and useless burden. The gospel is a proclaimed gospel. Thus, a sermon is never a sermon until it is delivered. A minister is never a preacher until he communicates his message to others.

The great preachers of Christian history, without exception, have been effective in the delivery of sermons. This does not mean that each was an orator, had a magnificent voice, or had dramatic skill. It does mean that all have had the ability to communicate with their audiences. In this sense the delivery of the sermon may be considered correctly to be an index of the spiritual power of both the man who preaches and of the Christian community.

In spite of the importance of delivery, it is often the most neglected area of sermon preparation. Many ministers who are diligent in other areas of sermon construction give little attention to self-improvement in delivery. Their rationalizations are legion: they have never heard themselves speak; they have no qualified critic; they are convinced that if a preacher has something to say, he will automatically say it well; a study of speech is too elementary for such a sacred task as preaching; it is impossible to change old habits.[1] The minister who is convinced of

---

[1] See Elise Hahn, *et al, Basic Voice Training for Speech* (New York: McGraw-Hill Book Co., Inc., 1957), pp. 3-4.

the centrality of preaching, however, will neglect preparation for delivery at his own peril.

A study of delivery involves a discussion of the minister's personality as it relates to preaching, the minister's use of his voice, the use of his body, and the styles of sermon delivery.

The Minister's Personality

The minister's personality is of such vital importance to the delivery of the sermon that it is not uncommon to read that the first law of preaching is "be yourself." A popular textbook in speech lists the following as one of the seven basic principles of delivery: "An able speaker is (1) an able person, (2) in good emotional state, (3) with a good attitude toward himself and toward his audience." [2] A study of delivery must look first at the relation between personality and effective communication.

The Minister's Emotions

In at least one area of personality the minister *is* himself in delivery, whether he likes it or not. It is inevitable that his emotions will be seen in his preaching. Delivery has its first residence, not in the mouth or in the body, but in the inner feelings of the speaker. What the speaker is and feels as a person will be seen and heard through his eyes, his face, his voice, his gestures, his posture, and his attitude toward the congregation. And if there is a conflict between emotion and statement, emotion will be most evident and most powerful. Therefore, "the most important thing in delivery is the man: what he is, what he thinks, how he feels, his motives, purposes, and yearnings." [3]

Emotional background.—The minister's total experience as a person is reflected in his delivery. His deepest feelings, his basic emotions and attitudes persistently appear in his preaching. This emotional principle in delivery has been called pathos. [4]

---

[2] Lew R. Sarett and W. T. Foster, *Basic Principles of Speech* (2nd. ed.; Boston: Houghton Mifflin Co., 1946), p. 26.

[3] Jones, *op. cit.*, p. 222.

[4] This is the term used by Dwight E. Stevenson and Charles F. Diehl, *Reaching People from the Pulpit* (New York: Harper & Bros., 1958), p. 77.

The minister's home, his church, his school, his associates, his total background—all of these have contributed to his personality and all are to be seen in his delivery. Such emotional factors as personality adjustment and self-acceptance have an unconscious but telling influence upon speech. A lifelong struggle with an inferiority complex because of physical problems or emotional insecurity may result in a timid or even a pontifical delivery. A desire to be accepted can rob the minister of his most vital asset as a preacher, his ability to "be himself." A background of defensiveness or fear may initiate an aggressive spirit which will determine the speaker's attitude toward himself and his congregation.

Also involved in pathos is the speaker's Christian experience, especially his motivation and security in the ministry. If his personal experience with God is not adequate and growing, it will show up in sermon content and also in delivery, particularly at the point of earnestness. If the preacher has entered the ministry for any reason other than divine compulsion and a response to human need, his delivery will almost inevitably reflect his inadequate motivation. His displeasure with the task of preaching will be evident. His dislike for people may be seen in his desire to punish or, quite paradoxically, in his overly effusive delivery. Uncertainty and insecurity in the ministry often influence delivery.

A student in a class in sermon delivery demonstrated in two class sermons that his preaching was almost totally negative and that he had a strong tendency to punish his hearers. When the teacher discussed these matters in a personal conference, the student immediately stated his problem. He was not at all sure that he should even be in the ministry! On similar evidence Edgar N. Jackson observes that "much that has been done in the pulpit has been little more than a projection of the disturbances and maladjustments of the preacher himself." [5] It is when a man speaks from a sense of divine purpose and conviction, as a person who has matured in his own emotions and as a con-

---

[5] *Op. cit.*, p. 177.

cerned friend of those who hear him that he can be most effective in delivery.

Pathos cannot be improved by mere desire or by mechanical techniques. To change this emotional factor in delivery, the minister must learn to face and accept himself as a person. Improvement waits upon personality catharsis. Every minister needs a counseling experience in which such catharsis occurs. Classes in delivery in which the student, in private conference, is evaluated at the point of pathos are invaluable. A trusted and capable critic in the congregation can also assist in the pastor's emotional security.

Emotional identification.—Another way in which the minister *is* himself in delivery is the manner in which he is emotionally identified with the immediate preaching situation. The factor here involved is his poise, his emotional stability in the actual delivery of the sermon.

Poise is often disturbed by fear. An ego concern, the size and attitude of the congregation, the occasion, objective, and content of the sermon, the presence of those in the congregation who demand a great deal of the preacher, and similar circumstances can affect poise. Lack of poise is clearly evident in the delivery of the sermon. Nervousness is seen in the flushed face, unsteady hands and knees, awkward posture or attention to the person, rapid and shallow breathing, a dry mouth and resultant faulty articulation, a strained pitch, the oral pause, and rapid rate. Extreme cases of fear can result in complete forgetfulness for those who speak without notes or in an absolute inability to speak at all for others.

It is an error to believe that all fear should be removed from the speaker. The minister who comes to the pulpit without nervous tension is unlikely to preach well. Tension is necessary to effective public speech. It makes for readiness, for zest in delivery. But if poise is to exist, fear must be controlled.

There are means of improving poise in the preaching situation. For one thing, the minister should be thoroughly prepared. The more familiar he is with his sermon, the less likely is his delivery to be adversely affected by fear. The minister can conquer fear by losing himself in a well-prepared sermon built on a truth from God which he believes with deep conviction. Closely related to this, he should have a deep concern for his hearers. If he is more vitally concerned with the spiritual needs of his audience than he is with their approval of him or his sermon, the preacher can better deal with his fears. Of supreme importance to pulpit poise is reliance upon God. One should prepare the sermon as if all depends on the preacher and go into the pulpit confident that the effectiveness of the delivery rests totally with God. Poise more readily belongs to him who delivers a word from God as God's prepared spokesman to needy men.

There are physical aids to poise also. Fear is in part physically related. It is the means by which the body is prepared for an unusual effort.[6] Thus, fear may often be relieved by physical means. The minister should relax his tense muscles while seated on the platform. Especially should he relax the muscles of his throat that he may speak at a normal pitch level. He should look at his congregation before he rises to preach. Direct eye contact with the congregation will build audience rapport and will lessen the poise problem. The speaker should breathe deeply as he approaches the pulpit. He should pause for a moment before beginning to speak and adjust his breathing to a normal rate. Appropriate body movement during the sermon will afford a legitimate outlet for the nervous energy which can otherwise hinder effective delivery.

Poise may also be affected by an attitude toward the specific preaching situation. One who is well adjusted emotionally may, for reasons other than fear, lose his poise in a given situation. An unfortunate attitude toward a given sermon or a given audience may be clearly revealed in delivery. The speaker's attitude toward himself or his personal fitness to preach affect delivery.

---

[6] The interested reader may find a detailed discussion of this matter in Harold M. Kaplan, *Anatomy and Physiology of Speech* (New York: McGraw-Hill Book Co., Inc., 1960), pp. 64-65.

Some insist, for these reasons, that it is always possible after a sermon to determine how the speaker felt toward his sermon, his audience, and himself.[7] The keys to poise are personal identification with the subject and the audience and physical and spiritual fitness for the demands of the pulpit.

Emotionally the minister, for better or worse, *is* himself. His delivery reflects his personality. In yet another area of personality the minister always *should be* himself, though often he is not.

The Minister's Creative Self

Delivery should be natural. The speaker should dare to be himself, without affectation, reflecting his own creative personality. The layman's most frequent criticism of ministers is that they do not speak naturally. They assume a "preacher's tone," a false piety, an affectation in the pulpit. Charles Haddon Spurgeon seems to agree:

Scarcely one man in a dozen in the pulpit talks like a man. . . . You may go all around, to church and chapel alike, and you will find that by far the larger majority of our preachers have a holy tone for Sundays. They have one voice for the parlour and the bedroom, and quite another tone for the pulpit; so that, if not double-tongued sinfully, they certainly are so literally. The moment some men shut the pulpit door, they leave their own personal manhood behind them, and become as official as the parish beadle.[8]

The preacher should not be an actor, either by preaching that which is not his own by conviction and preparation, or by a delivery which does not reflect his true personality.

Every principle of sermon delivery, whether pertaining to vocal production, use of the body, or delivery style, is to be judged by a more important concept—let the minister be himself. Let him be his improved self, to be sure. But, at all costs, let the creative endowments of his personality, those distinctives which can make him effective, be seen.

---

[7] Stevenson and Diehl, *op. cit.*, pp. 74-76.
[8] *Lectures to My Students*, pp. 111-12.

The Minister's Voice

The minister's most important physical instrument for preaching is his voice. He should be interested, then, in understanding, protecting, and gaining the maximum use of his vocal processes. Ilion T. Jones shares this conviction to the extent of stating that good care of the voice is a part of the obligation one assumes in accepting God's call to the ministry.[9] But some men abuse and neglect it so seriously that they must retire from the pulpit early in life. Many others never achieve the delivery power God gave them because they do not use the voice properly.

Even the seminary student should give maximum attention to the voice. During his earliest years in the ministry his vocal habits are developed. It is extremely difficult, though certainly not impossible, to change delivery patterns after a number of years in the pulpit. The young man should evaluate and improve his vocal production to the fullest. This raises a question, often debated, as to whether formal speech training is of value to the minister. Many fear that speech therapists "attempt too much" and give the minister an artificial excellence. This danger is greatly reduced with the contemporary emphasis in speech on conversational delivery. Those who have organic problems with vocal production certainly must have expert and often medical care. Those with functional disorders need the discipline of wise speech therapy. All ministers should have training in speech. In addition to formal speech classes, college courses in preaching will be valuable. Seminary classes in delivery will further the discipline. Upon graduation the pastor may continue his training by self-evaluation with the aid of a tape recorder, by participation in workshops in sermon delivery, and by using the services of a wise critic in his congregation. Good speaking voices are *developed*, and the minister must take advantage of every opportunity to train his voice as a God-given instrument for communicating the gospel. Why should those who use their voices for lesser ends be more diligent than the man with the Word?

---

[9] *Op. cit.*, p. 204.

It is not within the scope of this chapter to present a technical discussion of the voice. Such is available in many excellent speech texts.[10] A general summary of vocal production and voice problems must suffice.

The Production of Speech

The physical processes which produce speech should be understood. There are four such processes: respiration, phonation, resonation, and articulation. Each process involves the use of bodily organs in addition to speech organs. Thus, speech is called an *overlaid function*. Since this is the case, proper speech habits are formed by mastering the use of the organs of delivery.

Respiration.—Respiration is the act of breathing. Nothing is more vital for effective delivery than proper breathing. Such matters as steadiness of vocalization, projection, rate, pitch, phrasing, and poise depend in part on good breathing.

Breathing for speech is quite different from breathing for life's other processes. There must be a more controlled rate of respiration. Air must be inhaled quickly and quietly and exhaled more slowly and steadily. There must be a supply of air in the lungs at all times for proper phrasing and projection. Thus, breathing for speech must be deeper and better controlled than ordinary breathing. In contrast to clavicular and upper-thoracic breathing, in which inhalation involves the elevation of the shoulders, collarbones, and chest, breathing for speech should be diaphragmatic or abdominal.

The diaphragm is a muscle shaped like an inverted bowl which stretches across the body and serves as a partition be-

---

[10] A partial list of such texts includes Sarett and Foster, *op. cit.*; Harrison M. Karr, *Your Speaking Voice* (Glendale, Calif.: Griffin-Patterson, 1945); William C. Craig and R. R. Sokolowsky, *The Preacher's Voice* (3rd ed.; Columbus, Ohio: The Wartburg Press, 1945); Hahn *et al. op. cit.*; Kaplan, *op. cit.*; Charlotte I. Lee, *Oral Interpretation* (2nd ed.; Boston: Houghton Mifflin Co., 1959); Raymond G. Smith, *Principles of Public Speaking* (New York: The Ronald Press Co., 1958), pp. 291-364; Lester Thonssen and A. Craig Baird, *Speech Criticism* (New York: The Ronald Press Co., 1948); A. Craig Baird and Franklin H. Knower, *Essentials of General Speech* (2nd ed.; New York: McGraw-Hill Book Co., Inc., 1960); and the excellent text in preaching by Stevenson and Diehl.

tween the thorax and the abdomen. When it is used in breathing it is depressed, pushing downward and forward upon the front wall of the abdomen. The space above the diaphragm, including the lungs, is enlarged. Thus, the lungs gain a greater amount of air. Exhalation gradually relaxes the diaphragm to its former position, and air is passed silently from the lungs. One simple way to discover whether the diaphragm is being used is to place one hand on the chest and the other on the abdomen. If diaphragmatic breathing is being done the abdomen will move forward against the belt when air is inhaled, while the chest will remain passive. The use of the diaphragm is normal with animals and with small children, but the adult may be so unaccustomed to using it that he will need various exercises to breathe properly again.[11]

A constant factor in breathing for delivery is proper posture. The minister should stand comfortably erect but without stiffness. The head should be held so that the eyes are directed at the level of the horizon. A psychological feeling of suspension assures a posture which is erect without tension. In such a posture the speaker is able to do diaphragmatic breathing and to enjoy the vocal benefits of such respiration.

Phonation.—As air passes from the lungs through the vocal cords, or folds contained in the larynx, sounds are made. This process is called phonation and involves such factors of speech as pitch, range, and inflection.

The pitch of a voice is in part determined by the length and thickness of the vocal folds. The average length of the vocal folds in an adult male is said to be about one inch.[12] But length, as well as thickness, varies in individuals. Since sound is produced by air passing between the vibrating cords, this variation in structure results in differing basic pitch levels. Some voices are by nature higher in pitch than others. The minister with a high-pitched voice should not despair of effective delivery. Many of

---

[11] Excellent exercises for breathing are to be found in Stevenson and Diehl, *op. cit.*, pp. 43-48, 144-46; and Hahn *et al., op. cit.*, pp. 33-35.

[12] Craig and Sokolowsky, *op. cit.*, p. 43.

the most effective preachers have had such voices. The important thing is to learn to use the pitch well without abusing the throat.

Every voice has an optimum pitch level, referred to by some writers as the basic timbre of the voice. The optimum pitch is that which is the best or most normal for each person, dependent upon the structure of the vocal folds. It can be discovered easily, say Stevenson and Diehl.[13] Using a piano, the minister may sing down the scale as far as it is comfortable. Then he should go up the piano scale for five keys. This should bring him to his optimum pitch level. He may also find his basic timbre by lying down and, when comfortably relaxed, vocalizing the "ah" sound almost as a sigh. This sound will be near his optimum pitch.

The discovery of basic timbre is important because one of the most common problems of sermon delivery is a tone pattern above the normal pitch level. When the throat is tense, either because of posture, poor breathing, or nervousness, the vocal folds will be drawn tighter and a higher than normal pitch will result. If this persists throughout the sermon, the throat becomes tired and the voice hoarse. If there is chronic pain and tightness in the throat while speaking, and if a tired and hoarse voice follows, it is almost certain that the pitch is being strained. This problem is even of greater significance to those whose pitch level is normally high. The first steps in the proper use of pitch are to discover the basic optimum of the voice and to relax the throat so that this optimum can be the normal level of the voice.

The use of this optimum pitch does not preclude changes in pitch. Pitch must be varied if the voice is to be effectively used. But each voice has a proper range of variation, dependent upon its basic pitch level. Estimates of the normal range of the speaking voice vary from four to twelve notes on the scale. The most effective speaker will take advantage of both the higher and lower pitches in his range.

Changes of pitch are made for interpretation in delivery. If

---

[13] Stevenson and Diehl, *op. cit.*, p. 20.

pitch is not changed, a monotone results, and the force and meaning of the sermon are lost. A change of pitch on the tone is called *inflection*. There are three kinds of inflection: downward, denoting completed thought, affirmation; upward, denoting a question; and the double or circumflex, denoting by up and down movements of pitch an uncertain or doubtful meaning. A change of pitch between tones is called *interval* or *step*. Changes of pitch give proper melody to the voice and are essential to expressiveness. The minister should practice improving the pitch level and variation of his voice.[14]

Resonation.—Once the tone has been formed in the voice box, it is amplified and resonated in the cavities of the throat, nose, head, and mouth. The proper use of the resonating chambers gives tonal quality to the voice.

Some problems in resonation are organic and beyond the scope of functional speech therapy. A chronic sinus condition, for example, can result in persistent nasality. The shape and texture of the resonators have a great deal to do with the quality of the voice. Happily, however, resonators which are limited organically can be used effectively. Most of the vocal faults in resonation are functional. Most, indeed, are due to poor speech habits and can be corrected.

Problems of nasality are frequent in resonation. Nasality may occur either because oral sounds are coming through the nose or because no sounds are coming through the nasal passages. The sinus condition mentioned above or a severe cold usually causes the latter. Certain medications can relieve this organic cause of nasality. The resonating of oral sounds in the nose is almost entirely functional and is often associated with a regional pattern of speech. The minister is particularly guilty at this point because of "preacherisms," as well as regional habits. The "i" in the word "sin," for example, often is extremely nasal in pulpit delivery. So is the "e" in words like "seminary." It is to be re-

---

[14] Exercises are available in Stevenson and Diehl, *op. cit.*, pp. 21, 22-23; Karr, *op. cit.*, pp. 97-103; Sarett and Foster, *op. cit.*, pp. 213-14; Hahn *et. al.*, *op. cit.*, pp. 83-89; and Baird and Knower, *op. cit.*, pp. 122-24.

membered that only "m," "n," and "ng" sounds are exclusively nasal. Work on resonating vowels and consonants will greatly improve delivery.[15]

Some problems in resonation are closely related to phonation because they occur primarily in the cavities of the throat. One of these is harshness. When the muscles of the throat are tense, harshness results. Hoarseness likewise occurs when the resonators of the throat are not properly used because of tension. These functional problems can ordinarily be removed by relaxing the throat.[16] Breathiness is a half-whisper and half-voice quality which some use for dramatic effect in preaching. Occasionally it may be effective, but if it occurs as a habit of speech, it is offensive. Breathiness is generally the result of an inadequate opening between the vocal folds, partially destroying the resonating powers of the throat.

Articulation.—The final process in speech production is articulation. The organs of articulation are the tongue, teeth, and lips and are used to shape sounds into words. Clear articulation is essential for effective preaching. It has as much to do with being heard and understood as does loudness or volume.

Errors in articulation occur when sounds are added, omitted, or distorted. These may occur because of regional patterns in speech, "preacherisms," laziness, a failure to open the mouth, or other lack of flexibility with the organs of the mouth. Regional patterns may result, for example, in the distortion of vowel sounds or the addition of sounds, as when "Washington" becomes "Warshington." "Preacherisms" in articulation often distort sound, as when "God" is pronounced "Gawd," or "Jesus" is pronounced "Jeesus." Excessive rate, as well as slovenly speech habits, can persistently distort enunciation. Mannerisms of speech, such as the oral pause added to the front or end of words, can also mar articulation.

At least three things may be done to improve articulation:

---

[15] See Stevenson and Diehl, *op. cit.*, pp. 147-48; Sarett and Foster, *op. cit.*, pp. 216-18; and Karr, *op. cit.*, pp. 162-66.

[16] See Sarett and Foster, *op. cit.*, p. 213.

first, the powers of hearing should be developed so that articulation faults can be heard; second, greater flexibility with the tongue, teeth, and lips may be developed by therapeutic exercise of these organs; third, phonetics should be practiced, generally by a study of phonetic manuals, and specifically by constant work on the words which most often cause trouble.[17]

Rate

The rate of delivery is a vocal factor which varies properly with the speaker's personality, the size of the congregation, the acoustics of the building, and the nature of the sermon. Generally it may be said that the larger the congregation and the more difficult the acoustics, the slower should be the rate of speech. Some preaching objectives, as for example the supportive or didactic goals, require a slower rate of delivery. In no area is personality more determinative than in rate of speech. A good rule of thumb is: proper rate is varied and rapid enough to show vitality and slow enough to assure distinct articulation.

The pause should be used effectively. The dramatic pause, when not overdrawn, is an effective technique for emphasis. Occurring before or after an emphatic word or idea, it points the attention of the audience to the important ideas of the sermon. Changes of rate on words themselves, usually called *quantity*, add meaning and color to speech. The oral pause, a hesitation with an accompanying "uh" or "ah" is to be avoided. It often is a mannerism of speech as well as a rate problem.

Phrasing is the uniting of several words in a complete thought. Such thoughts should not be broken by pauses to breathe. The rate in which particular phrases will be delivered, as well as the length of the phrases, is a variant dependent upon emphasis, breath control, and size of the congregation and auditorium.

---

[17] Helpful exercises are available in Stevenson and Diehl, *op. cit.*, pp. 152-63; and in standard phonetic manuals, such as Empress Young Zedler, *Listening for Speech Sounds* (New York: Harper & Bros., 1955); and Charles Van Riper and Dorothy E. Smith, *An Introduction to General American Phonetics* (2nd ed.; New York: Harper & Bros., 1962).

Projection

Force is not primarily a matter of loudness. It is true that the minister should speak loudly enough to be heard in all areas of the auditorium. But loudness does not necessarily mean that the speaker will be heard. Loudness, indeed, may be a barrier to understanding. If it is excessive or incorrectly achieved by straining the pitch, it is both offensive to the hearer and damaging to the voice of the speaker. Projection is a better means of assuring force and understanding. The ability to project the voice depends upon the correct use of the diaphragm. In the discussion of respiration the diaphragm was described as being depressed in inhalation, pushing down and against the front wall of the abdomen. This affords a kind of resistance for the voice. Projection involves a stronger forcing of air from the lungs by means of this diaphragmatic thrust against the resisting abdominal wall. Projection affords a strong, round tone, not from the throat, but from this deeper source. When the minister learns to project his voice, he can speak with the correct volume and force without changing the basic quality of his voice or damaging his throat.

Variety as a Key to Effective Vocal Production

In several instances already we have hinted that variety is important to effective delivery. Now it should be said that flexibility in rate, pitch, projection, and force is the key to vital speech. A common problem with all speakers, but notoriously so with ministers, is vocal monotony. The fault has been so associated with the ministry that it has been called the "ministerial tune." It occurs when there is a pattern of melody, rate, or force which assumes a deadening sameness. Some have a monotone in pitch. Others have an inflection pattern by which every sentence is delivered in the same "tune." Others have a rate pattern which never changes. The answer to the problem is variety in every area of vocal production. As Blackwood has so graphically stated it, in the right kind of voice "the tone colors keep shifting as much as lights and shadows on a hillside in the afternoon, under a canopy of cirrus clouds." [18] Suitable variety is achieved when the preacher speaks naturally in such an animated way as to reflect the changing moods and meanings of the sermon. Such animated and natural speech is characteristic of conversational delivery. Conversational delivery does not mean subdued or "soft" speech. Rather, it means that the speaker, in the heightened force of platform delivery, is warm, personal, alive, and as natural as he would be in personal conversation. Such delivery, flexible in every phase of vocal production, is forceful. The audience *must* listen!

The Public Reading of the Bible

Every principle for the correct use of the voice should be applied to the public reading of the Bible. There is no more common weakness of delivery than poor reading of the Scriptures. R. W. Dale once observed that in all his life he had heard only one man read the Bible superbly.[19]

There are many explanations for this common weakness: the passage is seldom read aloud before the time of public reading; sufficient note is not taken of the mood and type of literature in the passage; the posture assumed for the reading limits the voice; the principles of oral interpretation are not known or followed; the passage is seldom marked for proper inflection, emphasis, or phrasing. Good reading requires careful study of the passage and the use of every vocal facility for effective delivery. The man who works with his voice in the reading of the Scriptures will have an appreciative congregation.[20]

The Minister's Body

Whether he has thought of it or not, the minister carries his body with him into the pulpit, and what he does with it there

---

[18] *The Preparation of Sermons,* p. 213.

[19] *Nine Lectures on Preaching* (New York: George H. Doran Co., 1912), p. 228.

[20] A full discussion of this subject is available in John E. Lantz, *Reading the Bible Aloud* (New York: The Macmillan Co., 1959); and in Stevenson and Diehl, *op. cit.,* pp. 83-97.

will prove to be either a significant asset or a liability to the sermon he preaches. The use of the body is indicative of personality. Even the almost "hidden" actions or appearance of the speaker give an audience an impression about him. Something about his attire, his posture, his mannerisms, his bearing may kindle a favorable or unfavorable reaction before he says his first word.[21]

Much more important is the conscious use of the body in the communication of the sermon itself. The mastery of posture and movement of the body is so vital that some have said that "no speaker can reach his maximum effectiveness—indeed, in many cases he cannot hope to reach even moderate effectiveness—unless he understands thoroughly the uses of bodily action."[22]

Key Principles for the Use of the Body

The correct use of the body for the preacher is that use which aids communication for a given occasion. This principle involves two important facts. In the first place, the correct use of the body is artless. It has been observed that if a perfect orator ever lived no one would know it; for a perfect orator is one whose oratory is unnoticed in the perfect communication of his message. So it is that good body usage is that which makes the body a vehicle of communication only. In contrast, the incorrect use of the body is that which calls attention to itself rather than to the message. There is no easier way to disrupt communication than by awkward or poor use of the body. One of the regrettable incidents of preaching occurs when the minister delivers two sermons—one with his words, and another with his body. One of the delights of an audience is to observe a speaker who speaks *with* his body and thus, by his total personality, transmits an idea from himself to others.

The second fact involved in the above principle is that correct body usage will vary with the minister and the occasion. It is an

---

[21] For a discussion of the "covert" use of the body see Sarett and Foster, *op. cit.*, pp. 135-37.
[22] *Ibid.*, p. 128.

error to insist that every speaker must follow certain stereotyped rules with the body. Correct body usage to a large degree will depend upon the speaker's personality, his audience, the occasion, and the content of the sermon. The minister must be himself. He will seek to improve himself because his "natural" techniques may hinder his communication. But in all discipline, he must remain *himself*. Some men, by reason of personality, will naturally use aggressive and unusual action in preaching; others would be most "out of character" in such action.

Closely related is the principle that correct body usage is based on inner motivation. Action cannot be planned in advance. This is not to say that it should not be practiced, but it is to say that in the pulpit the speaker must not be "chained" to gestures which he does not feel. Body actions must grow out of an inner impulse to communicate an idea. They must be based on convictions which are felt deeply and which a speaker desires others to feel. Building upon the thesis that the use of the body is largely a matter of mental attitude, Stevenson and Diehl advise: "Since the imagination of most people is perfectly healthy in conversation, all we need to do is to get speakers into the conversational frame of mind—not making a declamation, but talking with people about the things that matter, and doing it with a flexible body which unconsciously responds to the things perceived." [23]

The minister, thus, should be uninhibited in the use of his body. It is far better for a young man to overuse his body and later to temper his action than it is for him to develop an unnatural stiffness because he feels that the body should not be used in preaching. The most forceful delivery involves expressive action.

Appearance

The first view of the minister reveals his general decorum in dress and in the care of his person. This is one of those covert uses of the body by which he begins to speak before he rises to

---

[23] *Op. cit.,* p. 68.

preach. An unfortunate impression here can create a barrier to communication which is sometimes insurmountable.

Churches and denominations differ in what they consider appropriate attire for the pulpit. The minister should dress according to the accepted pattern of his pulpit. If it is customary for him to wear business attire, as in many evangelical pulpits, he should dress so as to call no attention to himself. Here is one of those places where the first principle of body usage is determinative. When attire calls attention to the speaker rather than to his message, it is inappropriate. A minister should be dressed conservatively and neatly in clothing which is correctly chosen as to color and which is correctly worn. To be careless at this point or in cleanliness of person is inexcusable.

Posture

A vital facet of body usage is the posture of a minister when seated on the platform awaiting the delivery of the sermon. He should sit comfortably but erect and preferably with both feet on the floor. He should be careful that his bearing indicates an alert personality, vitally interested in all phases of the worship service and in the people to whom he will speak. By all means he should avoid mannerisms which indicate a lack of poise. Nervous movements with the hands, frantic attention to notes, a failure to look at the congregation—all these indicate a lack of poise and are to be avoided.

Good posture while speaking is of importance both because it aids communication visually and because, as noted earlier, it enables the speaker to breathe properly and to project the voice effectively. Desirable posture will vary to some degree with the personality, but it is always that posture which best conveys the impression of poise and ease, while affording the erect bearing which aids vocal production. The weight of the body should be distributed evenly on the feet. It is good to place one foot slightly in front of the other to prohibit swaying of the body while speaking and to make it possible to change positions without awkwardness.

Eye Contact

No use of the body while speaking is of greater importance than eye contact. The preacher should draw an invisible line from his eyes to the eyes of his hearers and keep that line tight throughout the sermon, except for moments when he permits the audience to "rest." Good eye contact lets the eyes move over the entire congregation, not pausing too long with any one person or area.

In a large auditorium it is, of course, impossible to look directly at individual persons. However, if the minister looks directly at individuals in all areas of the audience, from time to time scanning the entire crowd, he will leave the impression that he is looking at each individual listener.

At all costs, the effective speaker eliminates objectionable habits with eye contact. Some of these mannerisms are: looking to the corners of the room, looking down at the pulpit floor, and looking slightly above the heads of the hearers without ever really seeing the people. These habits can and should be corrected. Even if a full manuscript is used in the pulpit, the minister can be so familiar with it that his eye contact, though not unbroken as if he spoke without notes, can be sufficient and effective. Good eye contact speaks of empathy and sincerity and is born of a desire to communicate. No other use of the body will pay such dividends in audience attention and response.

Facial Expression

If eye contact is the most vital use of the body, facial expression is the most neglected physical action. The face has tremendous potential for expressing the changing moods and meanings of the sermon. But many never adequately permit the face to express their inner feelings. Some have facial mannerisms, such as a continual smile or a constant frown, which are unchanged no matter what the mood of the sermon. The result is that an audience may doubt the sincerity of the speaker, or feel that he is belligerent, or miss the meaning of his words altogether.

It is difficult to work on facial expression, although practice

before a mirror can be helpful. Facial expression in the pulpit
should not be planned. If the minister should have the advantage
of seeing himself preach on film, either in a delivery class or in
his own pulpit, he will certainly learn of his faults in facial expression. But correction can never be mechanical. Facial expression must come from within. Therefore, the best method of
improvement in this area is a willingness to be uninhibited in the
expression of the deepest feelings. Again, a desire to communicate and the ability to speak with the animation of conversation
are essential aids to improvement.

The Gesture

It is customary to think of the gestures as the use of arms and
hands in speaking. Actually a speaker gestures with the eyes, the
head, the shoulders, with all the body, but the hands and arms
are used primarily.

Most speech authorities recognize the following general principles for the use of the gesture. (1) The gesture, like every
other action of the body, must be motivated from within. Thus,
the frequency of gesture will vary from speaker to speaker.
(2) The gesture should be made smoothly. It should involve a
"flowing" or co-ordinated use of the entire body. Gestures are
awkward when they are detached or abrupt. (3) The gesture
should be properly timed. It should precede the point of emphasis by a split second, so nearly simultaneous with it that the
audience hears the emphasis and sees the action as one impression. The poorly timed gesture may disrupt communication.
(4) The gesture should be appropriate to the occasion, the size
of the congregation, and the nature of the sermon. Gestures
speak of varying emotions by type and plane. Care should be
taken to associate gestures and meaning intended. (5) Gestures
should be varied. Some preachers use the same gestures again
and again, regardless of the ideas they wish to convey. The
result is that their gestures are without meaning.[24]

---

[24] Excellent exercises in the proper choice and use of gestures may be found
in Sarett and Foster, *op. cit.*, pp. 180-84; and Smith, *op. cit.*, pp. 321-22.

There are four *conventional* gestures, so-called because they are the basic hand and arm movements from which all other gestures are derived. The index-finger gesture is one of location and mild emphasis. The clenched fist denotes dramatic and strong emphasis. The palm-up gesture reflects an affirmative and even pleading emotion. The palm-down gesture displays disapproval, rejection, even contempt. Descriptive gestures, which are variations and combinations of the conventional actions, are as infinite as the moods they communicate.

There are three planes of gestures. The upper plane, which is the area from the shoulder up, speaks of the most powerful and reverent thought. The middle plane, from the shoulders to the waist, is the area which will be used most frequently because in it all the basic emotions can be expressed adequately. The lower plane is the area below the waist in which the most negative thoughts are expressed. This area is seldom used by the minister because it is usually hidden from the audience by the pulpit.

If the speaker masters the options at his disposal in the types and planes of gestures, puts them into his disciplined self-consciousness by practice, and speaks without inhibition and with a consuming desire to communicate, he will be both varied and effective in their use.

General Body Movement

A final word should be said about general body movement in the pulpit. The key to successful communication at this point is that every movement of the body should have meaning. The minister should be himself, being careful that he neither overworks nor feels inhibited about a change of position or other movement. Too much movement generally detracts from the sermon. But changes of position are both normal and effective. A slight change in position, for example, can be most effective at the points of transition in the sermon. If a microphone or television camera is being used, however, the minister must be extremely cautious that he does not move excessively.

Mannerisms with general body movement should be avoided. Such habits as nervous tugging at the clothing, removing and replacing the glasses, moving the head in some regular pattern, thrusting the hands into pockets, constantly folding the hands in front of or behind the body, leaning on the pulpit, pacing about the platform without meaning, or, by contrast, remaining stiffly rigid in the pulpit—these often distract attention as much as mannerisms with the voice. It is neither possible nor desirable for a speaker to eliminate all personal delivery characteristics, but pulpit patterns which interfere with communication should be detected and eliminated from the delivery. He might occasionally speak before a large mirror; always he can be alert to suggestions from his wife or other friendly critic.

The Minister's Style of Delivery

Preaching should be regarded as a thrilling adventure. For the minister who delights in the work of the pulpit, no moment can compare with the time he stands before the people to preach. Here is the creative moment when he speaks for God and when men confront God. If this moment is priceless, the preacher will always be in search of those methods which will best enable him to speak to the people. His discovery of the most effective style of delivery is primary in that search.

Many opinions as to the most effective means of delivery have been offered. The debate has often waxed warm. One says, for example, that "the use of notes is heartily recommended only for the dull or lazy minister." [25] Another replies that for him to preach without notes would only increase his temptation to use "trite phrases," "oft-repeated illustrations," "worn-out perorations," and "theological gobbledygook." [26] So goes the argument! Before the student makes a personal choice of delivery style, he should understand and examine the merits of each of his options.

---

[25] M. F. Ewton, "Why I Preach Without Notes," *The Baptist Program* (October, 1958), p. 14.

[26] Charles Wellborn, "Preaching with Notes Is Most Effective for Me!" *The Baptist Program* (March, 1959), p. 41.

Reading the Manuscript

The manuscript method of sermon delivery demands the preparation of a full manuscript to be read from the pulpit. It has been used by many successful and dynamic preachers, including Jonathan Edwards, Horace Bushnell, John Henry Jowett, and Henry Van Dyke.

There are obvious advantages in the use of manuscript delivery. It demands the fullest preparation. As we have already noted, there is no discipline in sermon preparation more valuable than writing. Writing forces the minister to consider his style as well as his content. It is of particular value to the young minister. A second advantage of the manuscript method is that the sermon is delivered as planned. Regardless of his physical condition or of other distractions, the minister who speaks from a manuscript presents his sermon without unfortunate omission. Again, the reading of the sermon assures fuller use of and accurate quotation of supporting material. The style of the sermon, carefully prepared in writing, will not be lost in the moment of delivery. With these assurances, the preacher can approach the pulpit without undue tension.

The disadvantages of reading the sermon are also obvious. Perhaps the most frequently mentioned criticism of this style is that it is less likely to afford maximum audience rapport. Unless the minister is unusually gifted in reading or is so familiar with his manuscript that he does not actually read it fully (in which case, he is not actually using the manuscript method), it is difficult for him to establish good eye contact with the congregation or to respond to the minister-audience exchange which makes for vital delivery. Again, the sermon may be less forceful when read because it appears to be wooden or presented without conviction. Webb Garrison denies, however, that the use of a manuscript invariably means that the attention of the audience is drawn away from the message. He states that the claim of many homiletic texts that such is the case "has not been substantiated by actual tests." [27]

---

[27] *Op. cit.*, p. 86.

Delivery may be weakened in reading also because facial expressions and quality of voice can be affected by the posture of the head and body usually made necessary. Finally, the minister who relies on his manuscript exclusively for a long period of time may find that he is unable to speak effectively by any other style. This would appear to severely limit his potential as a speaker.

Thus, the effective reading of a manuscript in the pulpit is probably reserved for those who have an unusual talent. If the method is chosen, let the art of delivery by reading be mastered. Broadus insists that a sermon delivered in this style should be read and not preached, for he feels that the attempt to "convert reading into speaking" is doomed to failure.[28] One is more prone to agree with Bowie, however, that such a sermon can and should be preached and not merely read.[29] Such is made possible by an identity with the sermon and by a mastery of essential delivery techniques.

Preaching from Memory

The memory method of sermon delivery differs from the manuscript method only in that a prepared manuscript is memorized and delivered verbatim without notes. This method has every advantage of the manuscript method with the addition of greater audience contact and resultant force in delivery. The minister who memorizes easily and speaks naturally from memory can attain heights of rhetorical excellence in the pulpit which are enviable.

Potential disadvantages of the memory method are numerous. The speaker may find that his mind is so occupied with the task of remembering the exact wording of the sermon that he cannot respond to his audience in the way necessary for persuasive preaching. The delivery of the memorized sermon can be artificial and empty of voice variation essential to animation. The

---

[28] *On the Preparation and Delivery of Sermons*, p. 320.

[29] Walter Russell Bowie, *Preaching* (New York: Abingdon Press, 1954), p. 207.

threat of forgetfulness is so severe that excessive nervousness may result. Any distraction in the congregation can interrupt the memory with disastrous results. Delivery may well depend to an excessive degree upon the minister's physical and mental well-being. Finally, the memorizing of manuscripts, especially for those who preach twice on Sunday and at other stated times in the week, may prove to be too time-consuming.

As was noted with the manuscript method, delivery from memory is likely reserved for those who have an unusual ability. The powers of memory are not equal with all men. Although all ministers should develop memory to the fullest extent, some will never possess the ability to preach by this method as well as others. Those who find that they can adopt the style should be prepared to give unlimited time to preparation and should master the art of speaking naturally from memory. The memorized sermon must be a sermon, not a declamation!

Impromptu Delivery

By the use of the impromptu style of delivery, the minister literally speaks out of the "overflow," that is, he speaks without specific and detailed preparation. Doubtless some men have read so extensively and have had such unusual power of recall and analysis, that they have been able to preach effectively by this method. Such men, however, are rare.

On some occasions every minister will excel in a sermon which he is forced to deliver "on the spot," especially if the demand is accompanied by unusual emotions. He should never be tempted to believe, after such an experience, that he should always so speak. Those who insist that the preacher should simply permit "the Holy Spirit to fill his mouth" severely limit the Spirit's power. They seem to overlook the fact that the Holy Spirit can deal with the preacher in his study as well as in the pulpit. He is in need of the Spirit in both places.

The impromptu method is of such limited usefulness and is accompanied by such obvious weakness that it can be quickly dismissed as an adopted style of sermon delivery.

Extemporaneous Preaching

The most prevalent method of sermon delivery is extemporaneous. It is that method by which the sermon is prepared in a brief or annotated outline, and notes are used in preaching. It is here called "extemporaneous" because the speaker prepares, but not to the fullest extent. He knows what he will say, but he does not know how it will be said. He organizes his thoughts, usually strengthens them with quotations, biblical references, illustrations, and other material, but he does not mature his style to the point of writing in full. He is familiar with the sermon, but he has not become so familiar with it that he can deliver it without notes.

The extemporaneous style has many advantages. For many, its greatest asset is that it is less time-consuming. This is an important item for those who are expected to be proficient in the multiple aspects of the contemporary ministry. A second highly acclaimed advantage is that the use of notes gives the speaker security in the pulpit while at the same time leaving him free to think creatively on his feet and to respond to the stimulation of his congregation. It is also apparent that the use of notes can result in more accurate utilization of sermon material. Scripture references, quotations, statistics, poetry, and illustrations can be delivered without error or omission. It is likely also that the preacher will "stay with" his sermon. The method should encourage him to speak naturally. He does not run the risk of becoming artificial in delivering a memorized "declamation" or in reading a sermon. These and other advantages were so much in evidence in testing audience reaction to student speeches that a noted speech authority states that "more 'good' speakers used notes than 'poor' ones." [30]

The extemporaneous style has been criticized, however, at several points. The fact that it costs less in time and labor of preparation may prove to be its greatest weakness. Some who use this method will never discipline themselves to the full ma-

---

[30] Alan H. Monroe, in *Measurement and Analysis of Audience Reaction to Student Speakers,* quoted by Garrison, *op. cit.,* p. 86.

turing of sermons. As a result, they may grow repetitive and trite in language and material. Whether or not this is a just criticism admittedly depends upon the individual. It is certainly not true of all who speak from notes.

The use of notes may hinder force in preaching. Eye contact may be constantly broken by reference to notes. Blackwood observes that although ideally a speaker may use notes without calling attention to them, actually "few ministers can keep from calling attention to their use of notes." [31] Force is more seriously hindered by the impression often made upon the congregation that the minister is not adequately identified with his sermon.

Does one have to use notes to speak on a subject about which he has a conviction as deep as life itself? An attorney will not likely refer to notes in his last statement to the jury, in which he seeks to save the life of his client. A salesman will not likely use notes in his effort to sell his product. Such facts force the admission that from the viewpoint of force, preaching with notes, although a practical necessity with some, is not the ideal in communication. Broadus insists that the use of extensive quotations, usually presented as a key advantage of extemporaneous delivery, may well be a weakness. It is his contention that extensive and long quotations do not increase but sometimes "positively diminish the interest and impressiveness of the sermon." [32] He feels that ideas of others, acknowledged and stated in the minister's own words, excel extended quotations.

If the minister chooses the extemporaneous style of delivery he should exercise self-discipline at two points. Certainly he should prepare his sermons diligently. It would be well for him, particularly in his younger years, to do a great deal of manuscript or full outline work, although he may use condensed outlines in the pulpit. He should be sufficiently familiar with his material and should practice such wise techniques that his use of notes will not be distractingly obvious to the congregation.

---

[31] *The Preparation of Sermons*, p. 198.
[32] *On the Preparation and Delivery of Sermons*, p. 332.

Free Delivery

A style of delivery which has been acclaimed by many is free preaching. The characteristics of this delivery are: the preparation of a full manuscript; full familiarity with it, not by memory primarily but by identity; delivery of the sermon without notes.

The most ambitious advantage claimed for free delivery is that it has every advantage of other delivery options without their inherent disadvantages. Like the manuscript and memory methods, it affords the most careful preparation, but it does not limit audience rapport or pulpit freedom. Like the extemporaneous method, it demands creative thought during delivery and affords maximum rhetorical excellence while at the same time demanding more rigorous preparation.

For some men the beginning of free preaching has marked a revolution in their pulpit ministry. For example, one pastor affirms, on the basis of personal experience, that by daring to preach without notes, "every preacher can increase his pulpit power at least 20 per cent, and many can make their sermons 50 to 100 per cent more effective." [33] Speaking of the discovery of free preaching as a major factor in his ministry, Clarence E. Macartney writes:

> The first Sabbath at Prairie du Sac I knew my sermon thoroughly; yet I took the manuscript with me into the pulpit, and although I never referred to it, the very fact that it was there seemed to chain me to the pulpit. I resolved to try it without a manuscript. The next Sabbath, and through all the Sabbaths of the many years since then, I have never taken a manuscript or notes of any kind into the pulpit.[34]

No less an authority than Blackwood so identifies free preaching with biblical and Christian history that he suggests it as both

---

[33] Bruce H. Price, "Increasing Pulpit Power," *The Baptist Program* (January, 1955), p. 5.

[34] *The Making of a Minister*, ed. J. Clyde Henry (Great Neck, N.Y.: Channel Press, Inc., 1961), pp. 129-30.

the most ideal and "natural" method of delivery. He affirms that it was only after the Reformation that any number of "conscientious preachers" adopted any other style.[35] Such a strong recommendation is based on the belief that it is incredible to think of Isaiah, or Paul, or Jesus preaching from notes. To Blackwood free delivery revolutionizes the pulpit ministry because it restores preaching to a "heart to heart and eye to eye" encounter. This is the ideal of preaching at its best.

Aside from the demanding advantages just named, the claims for free preaching most often made are: it renders preaching more acceptable and challenging to the majority of listeners; it tends to permit the minister to adjust more readily to the occasion; it heightens his ability to think on his feet; it is an invaluable aid, like the manuscript and memory styles, in the preservation of sermons; and it affords the best possibility for fulfilling the essential functions of both voice and body in public speaking.

In spite of the arresting claims made for free preaching, we must admit the possibility of some disadvantages in its use. In the first place, it may be excessively demanding in time. While the sermon manuscript is not memorized, it is fully written, often revised, and "mastered." To write two or three manuscripts a week and so master them is next to impossible for some. This may call, at least, for some combination of free and extemporaneous preaching. Other possible disadvantages are: free preaching may be repetitive and trite; successful preaching without notes depends excessively upon the physical well-being of the minister; free preaching may become wooden if the speaker is not truly free; the accurate use of quotations is limited; the sermon's line of thought can be lost or important material omitted; and needed security in the pulpit may be lost.

If preaching without notes is to be done successfully, certain procedures are mandatory. Perhaps the most widely used book to inspire and instruct in free preaching is Clarence E. Macart-

---

[35] *The Preparation of Sermons*, p. 194.

ney's *Preaching Without Notes*. He lists the following secrets
of such preaching: the use of a careful outline and the logical
development of the subject; physical fitness; spiritual readiness;
the training of the memory; a willingness to use fewer quotations; begin with biographical sermons; and be willing to per-
severe in the effort to master the style.[36]

Personal Decision

After such detailed discussion of the options which are open
to the minister, the important question becomes: Upon what
basis can the individual choose a style of delivery for himself?

The young minister will likely want to experiment with
several styles in his search for that delivery which is best for him.
It is possible to vary and combine the delivery styles from time
to time. Simply because one feels more inclined to free preaching, for example, should not mean that he would never preach
with notes. Again, he may deliver an annotated outline without
notes when it is impossible to prepare a manuscript, thus com-
bining the extemporaneous and free styles.

The fundamental necessity is for each minister to discover and
use that style of delivery which affords him the greatest freedom
and effectiveness in preaching. It is an error to insist that every
preacher should preach by any one of the foregoing methods of
delivery. In the final analysis, John Henry Jowett's striking
comment is correct:

There are some questions about the sermon on which I am com-
paratively indifferent. Whether it shall be preached from a full
manuscript or from notes, whether it shall be read, or delivered
with greater detachment; these questions do not much concern me.
Either method may be alive and effective if there be behind it a
"live" man, real and glowing, fired with the passion of souls.[37]

---

[36] New York: Abingdon-Cokesbury Press, 1946, pp. 153-72.
[37] *Op. cit.*, pp. 170-71.

Epilogue

Every minister longs for power in preaching. He would like to know the power of a Spurgeon, who moved his congregations to deep contrition, the power of a Jonathan Edwards, whose sermon, "Sinners in the Hands of an Angry God," left men clinging to the back of pews lest they fall into hell. He covets the power of a Whitefield, whose last congregation followed him to the stairs of his house at Newburyport to hear him preach until the candle burned low in his hand. He desires the influence of a John Wesley, whose sermons influenced personal righteousness a century after they were preached.

But power in preaching does not come primarily from sermon preparation, no matter how logical and demanding the steps of planning may be. The reader who hopes for power from homiletic methods will put this book aside in disappointment. The "steps to the sermon" are methods which will assist the minister in the preparation of better sermons, but they contain no spiritual dynamic within themselves.

To have power in preaching the minister must believe in preaching. It is often said, "Churches can no longer be built upon preaching alone." There is merit in the observation, because there has always been more to the ministry of the church than preaching. But preachers must not lose confidence in the efficacy of preaching; it has marked every period of spiritual advance. Preaching is the proclamation of God's redemptive deed, and by such preaching "it [has] pleased God . . . to save them that believe" (1 Cor. 1:21). It is, indeed, a sacred moment when God's servant stands to preach, for in this moment God speaks through man. The importance of preaching warrants the diligent preparation recommended in this book. Power in preaching results from an expectancy that through preaching God will move creatively in the lives of the listening congregation.

Power in preaching rests upon the content of the sermon. Much which is called preaching is not preaching, if a biblical theology of proclamation is to be taken seriously. God has promised to empower the preaching of his Word. Preaching must be kerygmatic if it is to have power. Every sermon, though its objective be ethical or supportive, evangelistic or doctrinal, must be based upon redemptive proclamation. The preaching of God's Word through the written word is powerful preaching. No amount of style can supplant content in effective proclamation, though style is the necessary robe in which content is dressed. Thus it is that the steps to the sermon are meant to be means to an end, never the end itself.

Let the reader also recall that power in preaching rests upon the character of the man who preaches. Nothing empowers the pulpit more than Christian manhood. The minister may be a perfect homiletician, his sermons may sparkle with brilliance, he may even boast of "results," but spiritual power belongs only to the man of spiritual character. The office of minister does not make a man holy. Rather, a holy man makes the office effective.

Most important, however, power in preaching depends upon the Holy Spirit. No sermon can be delivered in spiritual power apart from the presence of God's Spirit. There is no conflict between preparation and the work of the Spirit. The preacher must prepare as if preaching depended entirely upon him. But he must go to the pulpit as dependent upon God as if preaching had nothing to do with preparation. The most carefully prepared sermon becomes ashes in the mouth of the preacher without God's dynamic presence. But if God is there in the moment of delivery, as in the moment of study, the sermon is reborn; it becomes alive with dynamic power. Only God can convict and convert men. Only God can endow the minister for spiritual usefulness.

The power of the Holy Spirit belongs to the minister who abolishes self. The Spirit of God is a stranger to the proud, self-reliant man. The minister must place no basic confidence in himself. He must take no side glances at his own success. Rather, he must forget self in his complete surrender to God. The power of the Spirit rests upon dedication to Christ. The minister must be caught up out of his petty orbit into the eternal purposes of Christ.

When the statue of Phillips Brooks was erected, the sculptor placed a Bible in the preacher's hand and the figure of Christ with his hand on the preacher's shoulder, behind him. When that figure becomes representative of the modern ministry, we shall preach with power.

Bibliography

ANGELL, C. ROY. *Iron Shoes*. Nashville: Broadman Press, 1953.

BAIRD, A. CRAIG, and KNOWER, FRANKLIN H. *Essentials of General Speech*. New York: McGraw-Hill Book Co., Inc., 1960.

BAYNE, STEPHEN F., JR. *Enter with Joy*. Greenwich, Conn.: The Seabury Press, 1961.

BLACKWOOD, ANDREW W. *Biographical Preaching for Today*. New York: Abingdon Press, 1954.

_____. *The Preparation of Sermons*. New York: Abingdon-Cokesbury Press, 1948.

_____. (comp.). *The Protestant Pulpit*. New York: Abingdon-Cokesbury Press, 1947.

_____ (ed.). *Special-Day Sermons for Evangelicals*. Great Neck, N.Y.: Channel Press, Inc., 1961.

BLIZZARD, SAMUEL W. "The Roles of the Rural Parish Minister, the Protestant Seminaries, and the Sciences of Social Behavior," *Religious Education*, L (November-December, 1955), 383-92.

BOSLEY, HAROLD A. "Is Drinking a Religious Problem?" *Pulpit Digest*, XXXIII (October, 1952), 27.

_____. *Sermons on the Psalms*. New York: Harper & Bros., 1956.

BOWIE, WALTER RUSSELL. *Preaching*. New York: Abingdon Press, 1954.

BROADUS, JOHN A. *Lectures on the History of Preaching*. New York: A. C. Armstrong & Son, 1876.

_____. *On the Preparation and Delivery of Sermons*. Revised edition by JESSE B. WEATHERSPOON. New York: Harper & Bros., 1944.

_____. *Sermons and Addresses*. Baltimore: H. M. Wharton & Co., 1886.

BROOKS, PHILLIPS. *Lectures on Preaching*. London: Griffith, Farrar & Co., 1877.

BROWN, H. C., JR. (ed.). *Messages for Men.* Grand Rapids: Zondervan Publishing House, 1960.

———. "Power in the Pulpit," *Christianity Today,* V (January 2, 1961), 7-8.

———. *Southern Baptist Preaching.* Nashville: Broadman Press, 1959.

BRYAN, DAWSON C. *The Art of Illustrating Sermons.* Nashville: Abingdon-Cokesbury Press, 1938.

BUTTRICK, GEORGE A. *Sermons Preached in a University Church.* New York: Abingdon Press, 1959.

CALDWELL, FRANK H. *Preaching Angles.* New York: Abingdon Press, 1954.

CARROLL, B. H. *Evangelistic Sermons.* Compiled by J. B. CRANFILL. New York: Fleming H. Revell Co., 1913.

CHAPPELL, CLOVIS G. *Anointed to Preach.* New York: Abingdon-Cokesbury Press, 1951.

CLARKE, JAMES W. *Dynamic Preaching.* Westwood, N.J.: Fleming H. Revell Co., 1960.

CRAIG, WILLIAM C. and SOKOLOWSKY, R. R. *The Preacher's Voice.* Third edition. Columbus, Ohio: The Wartburg Press, 1945.

CRANFILL, J. B. (comp.). *Sermons and Life Sketch of B. H. Carroll.* Philadelphia: American Baptist Publication Society, 1893.

DALE, R. W. *Nine Lectures on Preaching.* New York: George H. Doran Co., 1912.

DANA, H. E. *Searching the Scriptures.* New Orleans: Bible Institute Memorial Press, 1936.

——— and GLAZE, R. E., JR. *Interpreting the New Testament.* Nashville: Broadman Press, 1961.

DARGAN, E. C. *A History of Preaching.* 2 vols. New York: George H. Doran Co., 1905.

———. *The Art of Preaching in the Light of Its History.* Nashville: Sunday School Board of the Southern Baptist Convention, 1922.

DAVIS, DENVER JACKSON. "How You Can Fashion Your Future," *Pulpit Digest,* XXXV (June, 1955), 35.

DAVIS, H. GRADY. *Design for Preaching.* Philadelphia: Muhlenberg Press, 1958.

DODD, C. H. *The Apostolic Preaching and Its Development.* New York: Willett, Clark & Co., 1937.

Ewton, M. F. "Why I Preach Without Notes," *The Baptist Program* (October, 1958), 14.

Flesch, Rudolf. *The Art of Readable Writing*. New York: Harper & Bros., 1949.

Forsyth, P. T. *Positive Preaching and the Modern Mind*. New York: George H. Doran Co., 1907.

Fosdick, Harry Emerson. *Riverside Sermons*. New York: Harper & Bros., 1958.

_____. "What Is the Matter with Preaching?" *Harper's Magazine*, CLVII (July, 1928), 134.

Garrison, Webb B. *The Preacher and His Audience*. Westwood, N.J.: Fleming H. Revell Co., 1954.

Hahn, Elise, *et al. Basic Voice Training for Speech*. New York: McGraw-Hill Book Co., Inc., 1957.

Hastings, Robert J. *A Word Fitly Spoken*. Nashville: Broadman Press, 1962.

High, Stanley. *Billy Graham: the Personal Story of the Man, His Message, and His Mission*. New York: McGraw-Hill Book Co., Inc., 1956.

Hoppin, James M. *Homiletics*. New York: Funk & Wagnalls Co., 1883.

Hurlbut, Jesse Lyman (ed.). *Sunday Half Hours with Great Preachers*. Philadelphia: John C. Winston Co., 1907.

Jackson, Edgar N. *A Psychology for Preaching*. Great Neck, N.Y.: Channel Press, Inc., 1961.

Jones, Ilion T. *Principles and Practice of Preaching*. New York: Abingdon Press, 1956.

Jowett, J. H. *The Preacher: His Life and Work*. New York: George H. Doran Co., 1912.

Kaplan, Harold M. *Anatomy and Physiology of Speech*. New York: McGraw-Hill Book Co., Inc., 1960.

Karr, Harrison M. *Developing Your Speaking Voice*. New York: Harper & Bros., 1953.

Kennedy, Gerald. "Pagans Have No Hope," *Pulpit Digest*, XXXIII (December, 1952), 21.

Kleiser, Grenville (comp.). *The World's Great Sermons*. 10 vols. New York: Funk & Wagnalls Co., 1908.

Knox, John. *The Integrity of Preaching.* New York: Abingdon Press, 1957.

Lantz, John E. *Reading the Bible Aloud.* New York: The Macmillan Co., 1959.

Lee, Charlotte I. *Oral Interpretation.* Boston: Houghton Mifflin Co., 1959.

Lenski, R. C. H. *The Sermon: Its Homiletical Construction.* Fort Worth, Texas: Potter's Book Store, 1927.

Lockhart, Clinton. *Principles of Interpretation.* Kansas City, Kan.: Central Seminary Press, 1901.

Luccock, Halford E. *In the Minister's Workshop.* New York: Abingdon-Cokesbury Press, 1944.

Macartney, Clarence E. *Preaching Without Notes.* Nashville: Abingdon-Cokesbury Press, 1946.

———. *The Making of a Minister.* Edited by J. Clyde Henry. Great Neck, N.Y.: Channel Press, 1961.

Maclaren, Alexander. *Sermons Preached in Manchester.* New York: Funk & Wagnalls Co., 1905.

———. *The Secret of Power and Other Sermons.* New York: Funk & Wagnalls Co., 1905.

Macleod, Donald. *Here Is My Method.* Westwood, N.J.: Fleming H. Revell Co., 1952.

Maier, Walter A. *Let Us Return unto the Lord.* St. Louis: Concordia Publishing House, 1947.

Maugham, W. Somerset. *The Summing Up.* New York: Doubleday, Doran & Co., 1938.

Miller, Donald G. *Fire in Thy Mouth.* New York: Abingdon Press, 1954.

———. *The Way to Biblical Preaching.* New York: Abingdon Press, 1957.

Moore, Robert Hamilton. *Effective Writing.* New York: Holt, Rinehart & Winston, 1959.

Mounce, Robert H. *The Essential Nature of New Testament Preaching.* Grand Rapids: Wm. B. Eerdmans Publishing Co., 1960.

Niebuhr, H. Richard, Williams, Daniel Day, and Gustafson, James M. *The Advancement of Theological Education.* New York: Harper & Bros., 1957.

PATTISON, T. HARWOOD. *The History of Christian Preaching.* Philadelphia: American Baptist Publication Society, 1903.

_____. *The Making of the Sermon.* Philadelphia: The American Baptist Publication Society, 1898.

PRICE, BRUCE H. "Increasing Pulpit Power," *The Baptist Program* (January, 1955), 5.

RAMM, BERNARD. *Protestant Biblical Interpretation.* Boston: W. A. Wilde Co., 1950.

RAY, JEFF D. *Expository Preaching.* Grand Rapids: Zondervan Publishing House, 1939.

ROBERTSON, A. T., and DAVIS, W. HERSEY. *A New Short Grammar of the Greek Testament.* New York: Harper & Bros., 1931.

SARETT, LEW R., and FOSTER, W. T. *Basic Principles of Speech.* Boston: Houghton Mifflin Co., 1946.

SELLERS, JAMES E. *The Outsider and the Word of God.* Nashville: Abingdon Press, 1961.

SHERWIN, OSCAR. *John Wesley, Friend of the People.* New York: Twayne Publishers, Inc., 1961.

SHOEMAKER, SAMUEL M. *The Church Alive.* New York: E. P. Dutton & Co., 1950.

_____. "The Church's Commission in Our Day," *Pulpit Digest,* XXXV (May, 1955), 41.

SMITH, RAYMOND G. *Principles of Public Speaking.* New York: The Ronald Press Co., 1958.

SOPER, DONALD O. *The Advocacy of the Gospel.* New York: Abingdon Press, 1961.

SPERRY, WILLARD L. *Sermons Preached at Harvard.* New York: Harper & Bros., 1953.

SPURGEON, CHARLES H. *Lectures to My Students.* Grand Rapids: Zondervan Publishing House, 1955.

_____. *My Sermon Notes: A Selection from Outlines of Discourses Delivered at the Metropolitan Tabernacle.* 4 vols. New York: Funk & Wagnalls Co., 1884.

STEVENSON, DWIGHT E., and DIEHL, CHARLES F. *Reaching People from the Pulpit.* New York: Harper & Bros., 1958.

STEWART, JAMES. "Exposition and Encounter," *Encounter,* XIX (Spring, 1958), 169.

STOTT, JOHN R. *The Preacher's Portrait in the New Testament.* Grand Rapids: Wm. B. Eerdmans Publishing Co., 1961.

STRUNK, WILLIAM, JR. *The Elements of Style.* Revised edition by E. B. WHITE. New York: The Macmillan Co., 1959.

TERRY, MILTON S. *Biblical Hermeneutics.* Grand Rapids: Zondervan Publishing House, 1956.

THOMPSON, LUTHER JOE. *Monday Morning Religion.* Nashville: Broadman Press, 1961.

THONSSEN, LESTER, and BAIRD, A. CRAIG. *Speech Criticism.* New York: The Ronald Press Co., 1948.

TRUETT, GEORGE W. *A Quest for Souls.* Compiled and edited by J. B. CRANFILL. Nashville: Broadman Press, 1917.

_____. *Sermons from Paul.* Edited by POWHATAN W. JAMES. Nashville: Broadman Press, 1947.

_____. *The Prophet's Mantle.* Edited by POWHATAN W. JAMES. Nashville: Broadman Press, 1948.

VAN RIPER, CHARLES and SMITH, DOROTHY E. *An Introduction to General American Phonetics.* New York: Harper & Bros., 1962.

VAUGHN, WILLIAM P. "Six Days for Labor," *Pulpit Digest,* XXXV (August, 1955), 20.

WEATHERHEAD, LESLIE. *That Immortal Sea.* New York: Abingdon Press, 1953.

WELLBORN, CHARLES. "Preaching with Notes Is Most Effective for Me!" *The Baptist Program* (March, 1959), 41.

ZEDLER, EMPRESS YOUNG. *Listening for Speech Sounds.* New York: Harper & Bros., 1955.